79

80

84

88

123

126

129

SUBSCRIPTIONS

SCINTILLA 17 can be purchased directly through
Amazon.com or Amazon.co.uk.
We hope in future to make back issues available
through Amazon, though as yet please email
subscriptions@vaughanassociation.org
to get further details.

*

WEBSITE

vaughanassociation.org

EMAIL

subscriptions@vaughanassociation.org

Submissions for *Scintilla 19*

Please submit critical articles on literature
in the metaphysical tradition to
prose@vaughanassociation.org.

Please submit new poetry for consideration to
poetry@vaughanassociation.org.

All submissions are peer reviewed

SCINTILLA

The Journal of the Vaughan Association

18

"Looke downe great Master of the feast; O shine,
And turn once more our *Water* into *Wine*!"

> Henry Vaughan,
> 'Religion'.

"God like a wise *Architect*, sits in the *Center* of All, repaires the Ruines
of his Building, composeth all Disorders, and continues his Creature
in his first, primitive *Harmony*."

> Thomas Vaughan,
> *Anthroposophia Theomagica*.

A journal of literary criticism, prose and new poetry
in the metaphysical tradition

Published by
The Vaughan Association

Published in 2015
Scintilla is a publication of The Vaughan Association

Some of the essays in each issue of Scintilla originate in talks first given at
The Vaughan Association's annual Colloquium held over the last full weekend in April
near the Vaughans' birth-place at Newton Farm near Llansantffraed, Breconshire.

ISBN-13: 978-1507550496
ISBN-10: 1507550499
ISSN 1368-5023

Published with the financial support of the Welsh Books Council

General Editor, Dr. Joseph Sterrett
Poetry Editors, Prof. Damian Walford Davies and Dr. Kevin Mills
Prose Editor, Dr. Erik Ankerberg

Typeset by Dinefwr Press
Rawlings Road, Llandybïe, Carmarthenshire, SA18 3YD
Printed by CreateSpace, USA

Dedicated to the memory of
Anne Cluysenaar

Contents

Preface

Scintilla 18 comes after what is undoubtedly a very difficult year for The Vaughan Association. We mourn the passing of both of its founders, first Peter Thomas in September 2014 and then the horrifying news a few weeks later of Anne Cluysenaar's murder. We feel it fitting therefore to dedicate *Scintilla 18* to Anne's memory and to prepare a special issue next year, *Scintilla 19*, for Peter. It was their vision in 1995 to hold the first Colloquium to commemorate the tercentenary of Henry Vaughan's death on 23 April 1695. Equally, it was from Peter and Anne's inspiration that *Scintilla* was first published two years later and has continued to explore the work and related themes of Henry Vaughan and his priest-alchemist brother Thomas (1621-66). These seventeenth-century identical twins were shaped by their Breconshire birthplace, its hills and groves, creatures, herbs, stones, history and myths, the magical landscape of the Usk river valley that imprinted itself so firmly upon their work and imaginations. In this issue, *Scintilla* continues to explore these vital questions of the environment and its relation to spiritual and physical experience, crossing the critical and creative divide to bring together the best literary scholarship, prose and new poetry both long and short.

Like their childhood home and landscape, the Vaughan brothers' experience of the civil wars, regicide and republican revolution, equally shaped their lives and perspectives. Both brothers fought in that war and experienced the loss of institutions of both church and state that resulted. The discontinuity and alienation that followed were traumatic. Defeated, the twins reinvented themselves, Henry as 'Silurist' and Thomas as 'Eugenius Philalethes'. Their writings reveal the connections between identity, adversity and the creative process, connections which remain central to *Scintilla*. This journal exists to explore such conjunctions, crossing boundaries between past and present, place and vision, the material world and our inner lives, between metaphysical experiences and language, between science, poetry and healing.

Scintilla 18 has a number of articles that will advance our understanding in important ways of Henry Vaughan as a writer and how he was read. Jonathan Nauman's essay engages with the difficult and largely overlooked importance of St. Paulinus in Henry Vaughan's spiritual perspective and devotional writing. Through careful close reading both of Paulinus and Vaughan, Nauman is able to identify which version of Paulinus Vaughan read, but also state with some certainty that the Silurist had become familiar with this spiritual writer from the ancient world at least five years earlier than previously thought. If true, this places Paulinus's spiritual influence at the heart of the first edition of *Silex Scintillans* (1650). Indeed the ease with which Vaughan moves through Paulinus's work suggests an alacrity and affinity with the saint's perspective that considerably exceeds other influences such as Anselm, Nieremberg, or Eucherius.

Philip West discusses his discovery of two translations of Henry Vaughan's Latin poetry in a miscellany book of John Chatwin, an otherwise unknown Cambridge undergraduate in the late seventeenth century. Little information is known about the immediate reception of Vaughan's poetry, and the discovery of Chatwin's verse translation gives an inkling of a wider audience and a sense of how Vaughan's poetry was being received toward the end of his life. Here the importance is the very ordinary nature of the manuscript itself. Chatwin, it seems, is 'a child of his times' translating these Latin verses into heroic couplets and interspersing them amongst topical interests current for the day, 'libertinism and drunkenness, the nature of male friendship, and the evolving role of poetry and the arts'. Robert Wilcher reflects upon Henry Vaughan's perceptions of nature and its creatures. 'Franciscan' in its sensibility, Vaughan's poetry diverges somewhat from the perspective of others of his time, like Donne, and has been championed more recently by current interests in the environment, weather, and the creaturely interconnection of the natural world.

Moving more widely to other poets in the metaphysical tradition, Noam Reisner explores the sacramental language employed by Robert Southwell where poems like 'The burning babe' create a mental experience that 'flattens' hard metaphorical images on one hand and leads to 'a deep sense of spiritual rapture on the other'. Reisner argues that Southwell's poetics stands at that point of rupture when divinity in the thing itself was giving way to an emptied representation or memory, a process that would ultimately usher in the secular world itself. Southwell's poetic language, Reisner argues, requires the reader to re-engage a sacramental experience not unlike the forbidden mass, where one holds the hard material object in contemplation at the same time that one moves toward its transcendent qualities, an experience that anticipates similar effects in Herbert, Crashaw and Donne. Jeremy Hooker offers a surprisingly similar reading of a more recent poet, celebrating hard visceral imagery in the poetry of Rowan Williams. Here meaning presents itself in uncompromising imagery expressed through the language of violent rupture and estrangement, forcing us to look beyond the surface to an encounter.

The poems for *Scintilla 18* were selected in the autumn and winter of a 'dying year' (to take a phrase from Alex Barr's poem, 'Ash'). That departing year was made all the darker by the tragically violent death of Anne Cluysenaar, whose poetry, as many *Scintilla* readers will know, has graced our pages and inspired from the start. Re-reading the poems we chose became for us an uncanny experience: each submission seemed, now, to negotiate that passing. Encountering in these poems the proximity of rasps and caresses, the need to believe that 'dissolution / is only the *verso* of dazzling annunciation', the 'unrelenting violence of life' that is the obligatory other of our serenity, and the 'quickness of life' new-born, we saw her life and death conjured everywhere.

This is not to misappropriate and straitjacket the varied poems in *Scintilla 18*, but rather to recognise how poems endlessly rehistoricise and dehistoricise themselves. We dedicate the selection of poems in this issue to Anne's memory, knowing that the contributors' stringent perceptions of the material world – what Richard Berengarten calls the '*thisness here*' – together with their wider speculations as to 'where matter / ends, where the spirit begins' (Sean Street) would have pleased her. We particularly celebrate the ability these poems have in their lyric, dramatic and ekphrastic modes to resist the doctrinal even as they take up robust positions vis-à-vis a world replete with both 'geometries / of bounty' and 'wounds unhealed'.

"Classicism and Conversion: The Role of the Poems and Letters of St. Paulinus of Nola in Henry Vaughan's Silex Scintillans"

JONATHAN NAUMAN

Only a few of Henry Vaughan's published readers have chosen to address at length the devotional exposition on "Primitive Holiness, Set forth in the LIFE of blessed PAULINUS, The most Reverend, and Learned BISHOP of NOLA,"[1] a rapt hagiography with which Vaughan concludes his prose translations in *Flores Solitudinis* (1654). Each of these few readers, however, has tended to agree that this piece has unique resonance, in some way seeming to reveal more clearly than any other of Vaughan's extant prose works the center of his spiritual sensibility. Louise Imogen Guiney, in the preface to her pioneering scholarly edition of excerpts from Vaughan's devotional manuals, observed that this "Life" testified to a "cult" for St. Paulinus on Vaughan's part analogous with Paulinus's "own cult for St. Felix": "in becoming a biographer," she said, Vaughan "chose a subject of which he was full"[2]; Canon F. E. Hutchinson, following up on Miss Guiney's research, brought Vaughan's and Paulinus's common life circumstances and sensibilities into focus, particularly noting "that Paulinus not only turned to the religious life but also devoted himself to the composition of sacred poetry."[3] More recently, Kenneth Friedenreich has presented the "Life of Paulinus" as a nexus for Vaughan's transformation of his pastoral retirement theme from secular to sacred,[4] Mary Jane Doherty has

---

1 L. C. Martin, ed., *The Works of Henry Vaughan*, 2nd ed. Oxford English Texts [OET] (Oxford: Clarendon Press, 1957), p. 337. All quotations below from Vaughan's prose works refer to this edition. Citations from Vaughan's poetic works below are to Alan Rudrum, ed., *Henry Vaughan: The Complete Poems*, rev. ed., Harmondsworth, Middlesex: Penguin Books, 1983.

2 L. I. Guiney, ed., *The Mount of Olives and Primitive Holiness set forth in the Life of Paulinus Bishop of Nola By Henry Vaughan, Silurist* (London: Henry Frowde, Oxford University Press, 1902), p. xii.

3 F. E. Hutchinson, *Henry Vaughan: A Life and Interpretation* (Oxford: Clarendon Press, 1947), p. 134. This text will be cited below as *Life*.

4 Kenneth Friedenreich, *Henry Vaughan* (Boston: Twayne, 1978), pp. 111-119.

related Vaughan's testimonial acknowledgement of tensions between literary and religious value to his presentation of St. Paulinus as a character clearly resonant with his own "self-discovery and with antique authority for adoption of a certain public stance,"[5] and Philip West has called St. Paulinus Vaughan's "chosen model of ascetic piety."[6] As Peter Thomas has summarily observed, the "convergences" in the "Life" between Henry Vaughan and Paulinus "are legion"[7]; and he cites Jonathan Post, who provides perhaps our most searching and extensive consideration of Vaughan's patristic biography to date in his critical study *Henry Vaughan: The Unfolding Vision*: "Stylistically and psychologically, politically and emotionally," Post says:

> Vaughan was deeply implicated in his account of the life of Paulinus, to the point of seeing himself through his subject's eyes. Not only is the "translation" the freest the author ever produced, one in which he frequently cuts, interpolates, and shapes the original to his own liking, but the saint's life and the poet's are in many remarkable ways mirror reflections of each other and meant to be viewed as such . . . The many alterations indicate a Vaughan intent not so much on making Paulinus in his own image as in remaking himself in the image of a saint.[8]

As will be seen from what follows here, I think that Post has rightly sensed that the figure of Paulinus came to hold a special position in Henry Vaughan's devotional regime, one that was central and even pivotal to his stance as a sacred poet. While the shape of Vaughan's religious sensibility was quite distinctively his own, receptively combining Scripture study, the poems of George Herbert, readings in hermetic medicine and God's "Book of Nature" in the beautiful surrounds of the Usk Valley, all of these elements are galvanized in *Silex Scintillans* by a rigorist tone and dynamic of conversion whose expression may owe rather more to the Letters and Poems of St. Paulinus than has generally been recognized. For an opening example, let us take a passage from St.

---

5 Mary Jane Doherty, "*Flores Solitudinis*: The 'Two Ways' and Vaughan's Patristic Hagiography," *George Herbert Journal* ["Special Issue on Henry Vaughan," Jonathan F. S. Post, ed.] Vol. 7, Nos. 1 & 2 (Fall 1983/Spring 1984): 25-50 (29).

6 Philip West, *Henry Vaughan's "Silex Scintillans": Scripture Uses* (Oxford: Oxford University Press, 2001), p. 174.

7 Peter Thomas, "The Desert Sanctified: Henry Vaughan's Church in the Wilderness," in Joseph Sterrett and Peter Thomas, eds., *Sacred Text – Sacred Space: Architectural, Spiritual, and Literary Convergences in England and Wales* (Leiden: Brill, 2011), p. 180.

8 Jonathan Post, *Henry Vaughan: The Unfolding Vision* (Princeton, NJ: Princeton University Press, 1982), pp. 140-141.

Paulinus's 31st Epistle[9], written to his friends and monastic emulators Aper and Amanda:

> Both of you pray, then, that the almighty Lord who has set rivers in the wilderness may transform my barrenness into water springs, that He may shatter and disperse my hardness of heart, and that He may turn this rock also into a pool of water. May He sprinkle me with the dew in which He steeped the mystical fleece of Gideon on the floor. For His dew is my healing. Pray, I say, that He may deign to enter my garden, and to order the north wind to rise and the south wind to come, so that my seeds may flourish under the impulse of those breezes of life.[10]

Here, in a quick succession of Scriptural images, Paulinus asks for interventions from God which Henry Vaughan's personae in the opening poems of *Silex Scintillans* actually experience. We have here the description of God shattering of the author's rocky heart in the volume's emblem poem, with the specific choice of "Silex" or flint borrowed from another of Vaughan's favorite devotional authors, John Nieremberg[11]; we have a plea for God's spiritual healing under a metaphor of dew that would seem to provide precedent for the "Infinite

---

9 Primary citations from St. Paulinus, here and below, refer to Heribert Rosweyde and Fronton le Duc, eds., *Divi Paulini Episcopi Nolani Opera*, Antwerp: ex officinia Plantiniana, 1622; reasons for accepting this edition as the one Vaughan himself used are given below. Cross-references will also be provided to the current standard edition of the works of Paulinus: William Hartel, ed., *Sancti Pontii Meropii Pavlini Nolani Epistvlae* and *Sancti Pontii Meropii Pavlini Nolani Carmina* [*Corpvs Scriptorvm Ecclesiasticorvm Latinorvm* (CSEL), vols. 29 and 30], Vienna: F. Tempsky, 1894 (CSELi = vol. 29; CSELii = vol. 30). CSEL's enumerations are those generally followed by Paulinus's modern critics and translators, but they often differ considerably from those of Rosweyde and le Duc. In the present case, for instance, the letter listed by Rosweyde and le Duc as Paulinus's 31st Epistle appears in CSEL as Paulinus's 44th Epistle.

10 "Orate ergo, ut dominus omnipotens, qui posuit flumina in desertum, conuertat aridam nostram in exitus aquaram, percutiat & interrumpat duritiam cordis nostri, ut hanc quoque petram conuertat in stagnum aquae. Atque vtinam illo nos rore respergat, quo illud mysticum in area vellus infecit. Ros enim, qui ab illo est, sanitas est nobis. Orate, inquam, vt hortulum nostrum introire dignatus, exsurgere Aquilonem iubeat, & Austrum venire, quibus auras vitales afflantibus germina nostra viuescant" (279; CSELi 377-378). Translation from P. G. Walsh, tr., *Letters of St. Paulinus of Nola*, Vol. II [*Ancient Christian Writers*, vol. 36] (Westminster, MD: The Newman Press; London: Longmans, Green & Co., 1967), p. 242. English renderings of Paulinus's Letters below are cited from this edition and from its preceding volume in the same series: P. G. Walsh, tr., *Letters of St. Paulinus of Nola*, Vol. I [*Ancient Christian Writers*, vol. 35] (Westminster, MD: The Newman Press; London: Longmans, Green & Co., 1966). English renderings of Paulinus's Poems below are cited from P. G. Walsh, tr., *The Poems of St. Paulinus of Nola* [*Ancient Christian Writers*, vol. 40] (New York & Ramsey, NJ: Newman Press, 1975). These three volumes of translations will be cited within my text below as ACW *Letters* I, ACW *Letters* II, and ACW *Poems*.

11 See Vaughan's translation of Nieremberg's "Of Patience and Temperance" (249.10-11).

sweetnes" of Vaughan's "The Morning-watch," in which the soul's reception of "divine grace and spirit"[12] is presented as a flowering plant in exultation: "This Dew fell on my Breast" (179, ll. 1, 7); and we have an anticipation of the soul's enlightenment at the end of Vaughan's testimonial poem "Regeneration," whose final stanzas and epigraph from *Canticles* (149-150) summon the "rushing wind" of the Holy Spirit in terms that, like Paulinus's, especially develop the horticultural aspects of the Scriptural text.

Before offering more examples of Paulinus's presence in *Silex Scintillans*, it will be helpful to clarify the bibliographical details surrounding Vaughan's access to Paulinus's works. Vaughan eased the task of his modern editors by opening his "Advertisement" for his *Flores Solitudinis* translation of Eucherius's "The World Contemned" with an explicit citation: "Heribert Ros-weyd *published this peece at* Antwerp 1621" (312). Rosweyde and his colleague Fronton le Duc, both Jesuits, released an edition of the Works of Paulinus under the same publisher in the following year, 1622. Both of these Latin texts, the Eucherius and the Paulinus, included Francesco Sacchini's "Vita Paulini," which supplied by way of translation much of Vaughan's "Life of Paulinus"; but since in constructing his own Paulinus biography Vaughan also drew "upon the Works and the notes"[13] from the second Rosweyde volume, we can be sure that he "had access to both editions."[14] Readers, including myself,[15] have been inclined to link Vaughan's interest in St. Paulinus with the poems added to *Silex Scintillans* in its second edition (1655) because the "Life" and the expanded collection of sacred verse were printed at about the same time. I should note, however, that all of the lines of influence I have just suggested from Paulinus's 31st Epistle indicate connections with the first edition of *Silex Scintillans* (1650); and as will be seen below, internal evidences seem quite sufficient to posit a probability that Vaughan's devotional reading in the poems and letters of St. Paulinus began not during his illness in the early 1650s, but at least five years before. The free composition of Vaughan's "Life of Paulinus" – for example, translating into verse some lines from one of Paulinus's poems for St. Felix's Day, then following Sacchini, then skipping to a compressed rendering out of one of Paulinus's letters to Severus, then pausing to descant on simi-

---

12 E. C. Pettet, *Of Paradise and Light: A Study of Vaughan's "Silex Scintillans"* (Cambridge: Cambridge University Press, 1960), p.121.

13 Martin, p. 723. As Martin notices (724-725), Vaughan's use of the 1622 edition is especially attested by the poet's translation at length of a passage from Rosweyde and le Duc's notes to Paulinus's Elegy for Celsus, a passage which enlarges on the Christian practice of burying their dead near the tombs of saints (354.31-355.11).

14 *Life*, p. 134, n. 1.

15 Jonathan Nauman, "Alternative Saints: Eucherius, Paulinus of Nola, and Henry Vaughan's *Silex Scintillans*," *The Seventeenth Century* 26, ii (2011): 264-278.

larities between Paulinus's and George Herbert's opinions on church buildings, then returning to a later passage from the letter to Severus[16] – the mode here clearly differs from the close rendering with brief and occasional interpolation seen in Vaughan's translations from Anselm, Nieremberg, or Eucherius. It indicates an especially comfortable mastery of Paulinus's texts, and probably a deeper devotional familiarity with them.

We know, then, the specific edition of Paulinus's works that Vaughan read. We may also surmise that Vaughan may not at first have been so strongly attracted by the figure of Paulinus. In his earlier classical verse, the Silurist clearly had some admiration for Paulinus's contemporary and teacher, the Roman aristocrat and nominal Christian poet Ausonius.[17] Vaughan's "Life of Paulinus," however, unambiguously sides against Ausonius in its portrayal of the two men's verse dispute over Paulinus's decision to sell his goods and embrace a life of Christian poverty (341-350). Vaughan at some point came to accept, not Ausonius, but Paulinus as his true spiritual father and poetic model, going so far as to imply in his epigraph to the "Life"[18] a relationship with Paulinus analogous with Elisha's relationship with Elijah. This moment came, I would suggest, after the death of Henry Vaughan's brother William from a war-related injury,[19] an event that all of Vaughan's modern readers have been inclined to connect with his redirection toward sacred verse. Paulinus himself in fact modeled this very transition for Henry Vaughan; Paulinus's decision to embrace a more serious Christian life resulted directly from the untimely death of his brother. In Epistle 20[20] Paulinus wrote to his catechist Amandus:

> My fresh grief at being sundered from my brother causes me deep anxiety. I know that he has been taken only from this world and only for a time, and that I must soon join him in the next world. The more genuine reason why I mourn his death is the realisation that all his acts and arrangements up to his death were in accordance with my sins rather

16 This particular sequence can be observed in Martin, pp. 376-377, 726.

17 Ausonius is named fourth (after Apollo, Orpheus, and Petrarch) in the lineage of river poets Vaughan constructs for himself in the opening lines of "To the River *Isca*" (39-41); and the "formerly written" *Olor Iscanus* also includes a translation of "*Ausonii Cupido, Edyl. 6.*" (72-76), in which poem the god Cupid endures a mock-crucifixion by unfortunate female lovers in a somberly humorous amatory Elysium. P. G. Walsh observes that Ausonius practiced Christianity as the established functional substitute for Roman paganism: "we may term him a Christian Roman rather than a Roman Christian; the bulk of his poetry proclaims his allegiance to and his pride in his descent from classical Rome" (ACW *Poems*, p. 22).

18 "2 Kings *cap.* 2 *ver.* 12. *My Father, my Father, the Chariot of* Israel, *and the Horsmen thereof*" (337).

19 *Life*, pp. 95-97.

20 CSEL: 36th Epistle.

than with my prayers, so that he preferred to pass over to his Lord as a debtor rather than as a free man.[21] (ACW *Letters* II, pp. 174-175)

Paulinus goes on to ask for Amandus to pray for his brother, whom he envisions in purgatorial suffering due to his failure to properly prepare for his death, and then requests intercessions for himself as well:

> Pray also for me, that I may not die in my sins. Pray that the Lord may give me notice of my death, that I may know my failings and hasten to fulfil what remains to be done. Pray that I may not be removed in the midst of my days as I weave a spider's web of useless works. Rather may my days be lived to the full, so that I die at a hundred and yet be still a boy, *in malice as children and in sense perfect*. And when I die, may I leave behind me repentance salutary by its good example to those who survive me.[22] (ACW *Letters* II, p. 175)

Every one of Paulinus's passionate petitions for a renewed and holy life resonates with the rigor of Henry Vaughan's sacred lyrics, the plea "to know my end"[23] in the first pilcrowed elegy, the thoughtful revaluation of the spiritual qualities of early youth in "The Retreat" (172-173) and "Child-hood" (288-289), the intention to "no longer cobwebs spin" in his rejection of earlier "Idle Verse" (204, l. 3). But most remarkable here is Paulinus's explicit connection of his brother's death with his own sins, a sentiment significantly similar to one Vaughan expressed:

> But 'twas my sin that forced thy hand
> To cull this *prim-rose* out,
> That by thy early choice forewarned
> My soul might look about. (170, ll. 9-12)

I think it very likely that Henry Vaughan's reading in St. Paulinus helped to shape his reaction to William Vaughan's death. Paulinus alludes to his loss in

---

21 "curæ nobis erat, ex recenti dolore fraternæ diuulsionis, quem etiamsi temporaliter ab hoc sæculo sciamus assumptum, in illo nobis citò consequendum; tamen ea veriùs caussa obisse lugemus, quia ex his quae gesta ab ipso in finem eius vel ordinata sunt, peccatis magis nostris quàm votis congrua egisse perspeximus, ut mallet ad Dominum debitor transire quàm liber (190; CSELi 314).

22 "ora & pro nobis, ne in peccatis nostris moriamur. Notum faciat nobis Dominus finem nostrum, vt sciamus quid desit nobis, & properemus adimplere quod restat; vt non reuoluamur in medio dierum inanium, texentes operibus vacuis araneæ telam. Sed dies pleni inueniantur in nobis, et simus pueri centum annorum morientes, id est malitia paruuli & sensibus perfecti. Ita fiet, ut mortui superstitibus exemplo bono salubrem pænitentiam relinquamus" (191; CSELi 315).

23 "Thou that know'st for whom I mourn," l. 57 (171).

three Epistles[24] and in one Poem[25]; and readers have gathered from these references that Paulinus's brother was murdered in his homeland of Aquitania by unknown assailants, and that Paulinus himself was accused of killing his brother: this happened when the Emperor Gratian, who had been friendly to Paulinus, was overthrown and assassinated by the forces of the next emperor Maximus, at which point Gratian's protégés were "exposed to attack from Maximus, who was prone to accept capital charges in order to confiscate the property of the accused" (ACW *Letters* I, p. 220). Paulinus would later see his brother's death, and the eventual failure of the ensuing false accusations, in terms of God's plan for his salvation, for the preservation of his life and goods enabled him to give himself to Christ and all of his goods to the poor. Vaughan's life would also change as a result of his brother's death; but he seems to have believed that, in his case, Paulinus's situation had been reversed. The brother in perilous spiritual condition had witnessed the death of a younger brother whose Christian faith was much more "pure, and steady" (171) than his own.

If, as I am postulating, Paulinus's Epistles helped to guide Henry Vaughan's personal understanding of William's death, readers should not be surprised that certain passages in Paulinus's Poems and Epistles would especially help to enable and inspire the poetic visions of *Silex Scintillans*. Indeed, Paulinus's influence on Vaughan's career as a sacred poet should be classified alongside Herbert's. As a poet within the English tradition, Vaughan was a professed convert of George Herbert, whose phrases permeate *Silex Scintillans* in densities scarcely paralleled in English literature. But we need, like Robert Wilcher in his recent examination of Vaughan's borrowings in his secular verse,[26] to take special care in defining the real mode of Herbert's presence in Vaughan's texts. I would simply note here that the manner in which Herbert's words are woven into Vaughan's sacred verses seems to me reminiscent of the use of Holy Scripture in Paulinus's allegorical meditations, in which the syntaxes of the Pauline epistles, the Psalms, and other Scriptural passages constantly crop up, sometimes seeming more relevant, sometimes less, apparently amidst efforts toward self-effacement, the merging of the author's voice with the Scriptures. Vaughan certainly understood Herbert's art, and he did make gestures toward emulating Herbert's forms and approaches; but Herbert's presence in *Silex Scintillans* seems in the end to be primarily spiritual and only secondarily literary. Although Herbert's new place in Vaughan's converted poetic lineage

---

24 See ACW *Letters* I, pp. 56, 220, and ACW *Letters* II, pp. 172-175, 334-335.

25 See ACW *Poems*, pp. 16, 389.

26 Robert Wilcher, "Henry Vaughan's Borrowings in the Secular Poems: Plagiarism, Imitation, Allusion," *Scintilla* 17 (2013): 11-27.

was most visible and proximate, it seems to have been imagined strongly within the line of Paulinus; in tone and bearing the poetic voices of *Silex Scintillans* often seem closer to the declamatory converted Latin classicism of Paulinus than to Herbert's disciplined parabolic simplicity.[27]

A good place to start our survey of highlight incidents from Vaughan's readings in Paulinus would be Paulinus's 4th Epistle,[28] written in the year 400 to his fellow Aquitainian and best friend Sulpicius Severus, a founder of Gallic monasticism and author of the *Life of St. Martin.* Paulinus includes in the opening of this letter an appreciative mention of a monastic haircut given him by Severus's courier, and this haircut then becomes the point of departure for a series of elaborate scriptural allegories. In the forefront, of course, is the figure of Samson – "it is pleasant to give free rein to words," Paulinus says, "and to follow the strong man of the Lord to his death so that I may weave an entire letter out of the subject of hair"[29] (ACW *Letters* II, p. 15); and so he does, delivering allegorical meditations one after the other, not only on the life of Samson, but on Nebuchadnezzar, St. Paul's teachings on hair length, the appreciative characterizations of lovers's hair in *Canticles*, the washing of Christ's feet and the drying of them with her hair by "the sinning woman in the gospel"[30] – that is, by the woman identified by other and later commentators with St. Mary Magdalene. One allegory generates another, and while considering the possibility that Samson's blind inner enlightenment at life's end was superior to his former physical ability to see, Paulinus delivers the following discourse on the Christian's relations with the world:

> To use one's eyes for the purposes of darkness, therefore, and to blind them to heavenly things by keeping them bent on things of earth, is to lose one's real sight. The soul is given clear sight to behold God by the blindness with which it holds the world in contempt. *For all that is in the world*, says Scripture, *is the concupiscence of the eyes*; and because of this the Apostle teaches us to close our vision to this world and open

---

27 My thoughts here follow Joseph H. Summers's observation that Vaughan "seems to have known *The Temple* (like the Bible) so well that his borrowings often are unconscious recollections, with Herbert's words or images put to surprisingly different uses or applications"; see *The Heirs of Donne and Jonson* (New York & London: Oxford University Press, 1970), p. 121. More could be said here about Vaughan's new lineage, which in fact extended beyond Paulinus to Hierotheus, the teacher of Dionysius the Areopagite; but the Dionysian strain in Vaughan's work requires separate analysis.

28 CSEL: 23rd Epistle.

29 "Sed vt totam de capillis texamus epistolà, iuuat indulgere sermoni, & illum Domini fortem usq; ad finem suum prosequi" (50; CSELi 170).

30 "illam Euangelicam peccatricē" (60-61; CSELi 182).

it to Christ, who *enlighteneth every man that cometh into this world* (that is, the mind of every man who comes).

The Apostle rouses us from our vision of immediate things to look up to eternal ones, saying: *Seek not the things which are in this world, for the fashion of this world passeth away.* And again Paul says: *Seek the things that are above, where Christ is sitting at the right hand of God.* In the words of Ecclesiastes: *All things under the sun are vanity.* And by the same token, truth lies beyond the sun. So, too, those who reside in the truth, though their physical dwelling is within the world, lie outside the world in their heavenly intercourse. Their spirit flies forth, and they mount and go beyond the dancing stars or the poles of the heavens; they rise higher than the elements, not being subject to material things or to the wearing of the elements. Their life is riveted to Christ and they are above the world, abiding in Him who is the blessed God over all ages.[31] (ACW *Letters* II, pp. 25-26)

When Henry Vaughan abruptly opens his persona's vision to eternity in his poem "The World" (227-228), he itemizes principal vices that keep men "bent on things of earth" and advocates "A way where you might tread the Sun, and be / More bright than he" (ll. 55-56). Here I suspect he offers an experiential sample of the sacred visionary posture Paulinus recommends in his own treatment of "the world" here. Similar dynamics can be observed when Paulinus's considerations of *Canticles* 5:2, "my head is filled with dewe, *and* my lockes with the drops of night" (A.V.) trigger allegorical examinations of the natural phenomena of dew and expositions on the spiritual significance of night. One feels the visions and emotions of Vaughan's "The Night" (289-290) and "The Morning-Watch" (179) ready to emerge when Paulinus suggests "that those *drops of night* in which Wisdom so gladly steeped His head and hair represent the saints whom Paul describes as shining amongst the stars, which on fine nights shine as the dew falls," and when he observes that:

---

31 "et ideò veri luminis damnum est, ad usum tenebrarum vti luminibus; & oculos in terrena defixos, cæcare cælestibus. Illuminatur aut anima tali cæcitate, qua despicit mundum, vt conspiciat Deum. Quia omne (inquit) quod in mundo est, concupiscentia oculorum est. Ob hoc Apostolus obduci aci nostram huic mundo, & enubilari Christo docens, (ei scilicet qui illuminat omnem homin venientem in hunc mundum, id est omnis hominis mentem venientem) sollicitat nos ab aspectu præsentium in suspect æternorum, et dicit: Nolite quærere quæ in hoc mundo sun:; præterit enim huius mundi figura. Et iterùm idem: Quæ sursum sunt quærite, vbi Christus est ad dexter Patris. Omnia enim (ut Ecclesiastes ait) sub sole vanitas. Proinde super solem veritas. Ita & qui in veritate consistunt, etsi intra mundum viuant habitatione corporea, tamen supra mundum sunt conuersatione cælesti et astrorum choros, vel cælorum polos euolantes spiritu scandunt, & superuadunt, celsioresq: elementis agunt non subditi rebus & vsibus elementorum, sed affixa in Christo vita superiores mundo fiunt, manentes in eo qui est super omnia Deus benedictus in sæcula" (58-59; CSELi 179-180).

now by the light of the Church, which shines with the entire reflection of the full moon, and of the holy men who are like stars in a cloudless sky, the good works of the faithful drip down in what I have called the night of this world. This dew gives life to the soul of each believer, and refreshment after the previous arid drought.[32] (ACW *Letters* II, p. 37)

Paulinus's gesture toward "the holy men who are like stars in a cloudless sky" seems to lead even more explicitly toward the images of Vaughan's elegy "Joy of my life! while left me here" (177-178), in which Vaughan considers his brother's continuing influence after death and proceeds to praise the helpful role of the saints in heaven for Christians still on earth. Though Vaughan had at least two biblical antecedents also for the image of holy men shining like stars,[33] the scriptural texts that use this simile do not imply any interchange between believers who have passed on and those still alive. It seems quite likely that Vaughan in making this connection[34] consciously followed St. Paulinus, who was indeed largely concerned to recount the benefits of saintly intercessions in his *Natalicia* – traditional Roman birthday poems[35] adapted to honor St. Felix, patron of Nola, each year on his feast day, January 14th. Take for example the opening of Paulinus's 11th *Natalicium*:

Only if the sky can forgo its stars, earth its grass, honeycombs their honey, streams their water, and breasts their milk will our tongues be able to renounce their praises of the saints, in whom God Himself is the strength of life and the fame of death. For Him they decided to barter their lives, and by their deaths to ratify the holy faith of nations

---

32 "Vnde intellegi datur, eas noctis guttas, quibus caput & crines suos sapientia maduisse lætatur, formam esse Sanctorum; quam & in stellis Apostolus coruscare designat, quæ æquè serenis noctibus micant, quibus rores cadunt . . . & nunc Ecclesiæ lumine quasi pleno lunæ perfectæ speculo, & sanctis hominibus, vt purissimis serenitate sideribus, opera fidelium, quibus animam suam quisque viuific s à præteritæ siccitatis siti reficit, quasi rores in hac (ut diximus) sæculi nocte destillant" (69; CSELi 190).

33 The passages at issue are *Daniel* 13:5 and *Philippians* 2:15; first of these was also alluded to by Vaughan in his 1654 Preface to *Silex Scintillans* (141).

34 Vaughan's elegy does not explicitly endorse the controversial Roman Catholic practices of asking for intercessions from the saints in heaven, or of identifying particular supernatural interventions as having been effected by the intercessions of a certain saint. But since the Poems and Letters of St. Paulinus heartily demonstrate and advocate both of these forms of piety, it does not seem likely that Vaughan strongly disapproved of them.

35 See R. P. H. Green, *The Poetry of Paulinus of Nola: A Study of his Latinity* (Brussels: Revue D'Études Latines, 1971), pp. 29ff. for a list of known Latin precedents for Paulinus's *Natalicia*, and ensuing descriptions of adaptations practiced toward his pagan models.

. . .[36] From the number of these princes Felix was appointed confessor in this city, and the fame of his name has flashed over the length and breadth of the world. But Nola has housed his buried body, and so takes pride as though he were her own star – for every martyr, wherever the region to which his body is committed, is both a star for that district and a source of healing for its residents.[37] (ACW *Poems*, p. 31)

Paulinus's surety of the beneficent influence of the holy dead over the living, presented here in terms of healing and starlight in the dark, resonates in its final imagery with the star "confined into a tomb" in Vaughan's most famous elegy[38]; and it would certainly warrant the terse transition between the first and second stanzas of "Joy of my life!", in which Vaughan places his dead brother William among the saints who aid the living like shining stars:

> Joy of my life! while left me here,
>   And still my love!
> How in thy absence thou dost steer
>   Me from above!
>   A life well led
>   This truth commends,
>   With quick, or dead
>   It never ends.
>
>
>   2
>
>
> Stars are of mighty use: the night
>   Is dark, and long;

---

36 Rosweyde and le Duc print the 11th Natalicium as a series of fragments, with this lacuna. CSEL and ACW supply the missing text as follows: ". . . mercarique sacrum pretioso sanguine regnum, / sanguine quo totum spargentes martyres orbem / gentibus innumeris semen caelester fuerunt. [. . . and to purchase the kingdom of the saints with that precious blood with which as martyrs they besprinkled the entire world and became the seed from heaven for countless races]."

37 "Sidera si caelo si possunt gramina terris / Defore, mella fauis, aqua fontibus, uberibus lac; / Sic poterunt linguis laudes cessare piorum, / In quibus & vitæ virtus & gloria mortis / Ipse Deus; pro quo vitam voluere pacisci / Et moriendo piam sancire fidem populorum / . . . / Horum de numero Procerum Confessor in ista / Vrbe datus Felix longè lateque per orbem / Nominis emicuit titulo: sed Nola sepulti / Facta domus, tamquam proprio sibi sidere plaudit. / Omnis enim, quacumque manet mandatus in ora / Martyr, stella loci simul & medicina colentum est" (626-627; CSELi 118-119).

38 "They are all gone into the world of light!", stanza 8 (247, l. 29).

> The road foul, and where one goes right,
>> Six may go wrong.
>> One twinkling ray
>> Shot o'er some cloud,
>> May clear much way
>> And guide a crowd. (177, ll. 1-16)

If Paulinus's sacred *Natalicia* yielded useful thoughts and images for Vaughan's commemorative elegies, Paulinus's single sacred epithalamium[39] provided a remarkable model for Vaughan's one marriage poem in *Silex Scintillans*. Paulinus's main concern in his poem is to differentiate the customs of the Christian wedding for which he writes from the secular wedding ceremonies of the pagan Roman culture. In "Isaac's Marriage" (160-162), Vaughan develops a similar contrast between contemporary popular trends in courtship and sacred marriage pursued in accordance with serious religious priorities, as demonstrated by the scriptural figures of Isaac and Rebekah. "This marriage must see nothing of the wanton conduct of the mindless mob," Paulinus maintains: "Juno, Cupid, Venus, those symbols of lust, must keep their distance"[40] (ACW *Poems*, p. 245). Similarly, Vaughan dismisses his own contemporary mob mentality, in which "bold-faced custom banished Innocence": Isaac had "no pompous train, nor *antic* crowd / Of young, gay swearers, with their needless, loud / Retinue" (ll. 20-23). Vaughan also follows Paulinus in his itemizing satirical gestures toward arrogant self-display in the "*rolls* and *curls*" (l. 34) of ostentatious hairstyles; in fact, one passage that emerges once Paulinus turns to sartorial advice for the groom seems likely to have provided Vaughan with his own poem's point of departure:

> If shabby raiment is an affront to respected persons, if proud hearts take pleasure in expensive appurtenances, then the example of our saints and the holy simplicity of our first ancestors must dispel such shame.
>
> Cast an eye on our parents of old in their abode in Paradise, for whom a single field comprised their whole world. Their covering consisted of sheepskins; are we now ashamed that our woven garments are spun from wool? When the beautiful Rebekah came as bride to consecrated Isaac, she was covered simply, with the veil of modesty.[41] (ACW *Poems*, p. 248)

---

39 ACW *Poems*, pp. 245-253.

40 "Absit ab his thalamis vani lasciuia vulgi / Juno, Cupido, Venus, nomina luxuriæ" (509; CSELii 238).

41 "Si tenuis cultus mentes offendit honestas, / Et pretio ambiri corda superba iuuat. / Submoueant istum Sanctorum exempla pudorem, / Castaque primorum simplicitas hominum. / Adspicite antiquos paradisi in sede parentes, / Quorum totus erat mundus, & unus ager. / Attamen his ouium pelles tegumenta fuerunt. / Nunc vti neto vellere texta pudet? / Pulchra Rebecca sacrum cùm sponsa veniret ad Isac, / Simpliciter velo tecta pudoris erat (511; CSELii 241).

I think it likely that this passage also led Vaughan toward the parable of his poem "The Ornament" (272-273), in which the intrinsic "native looks" of the "sheep-keeping *Syrian* maid" Rachel (ll. 15-16) shame a worldly crowd shopping for expensive clothing, "the latest modes of pride and lust" (l. 6). As Alan Rudrum has noted, "Rebekah is similarly praised" (615) in "Isaac's Marriage," meeting Isaac's servant at a well:

> in a virgins native blush and fears
> Fresh as those roses, which the day-spring wears.
> O sweet, divine simplicity! O grace
> Beyond a curled lock, or painted face!
> A *pitcher* too she had, nor thought it much
> To carry that, which some would scorn to touch;
> With which in mild, chaste language she did woo
> To draw him drink, and for his camels too. (ll. 35-42)

More could be said about Vaughan's response to Paulinus's epithalamium, as Paulinus's references to Isaac and Rebekah lead immediately into a contrasting consideration of the decadent spectacle of Salome's dance in Herod's palace, subject of another of Vaughan's Biblical meditations.[42] A compliment Paulinus directs toward the bishop officiating at his celebrated wedding, praising the prayerful man "as one attended by God's fragrance, as one whose face gleams with heavenly beauty"[43] (ACW *Poems*, p. 252) seems to me beautifully transformed and amplified in Vaughan's extended metaphorical description of the ascent of Isaac's soul in prayer:

> which so restored did fly
> Above the stars, a track unknown, and high,
> And in her piercing flight perfumed the air
> Scattering the *myrrh*, and incense of thy prayer. (ll. 49-52)[44]

These highlights represent the more obvious cases of Vaughan's poems benefiting from his devotion to St. Paulinus and to St. Paulinus's writings. I have kept to noticeable echoes in the poetry of *Silex Scintillans*, not pursuing the considerable influence of Paulinus's transformed literary vocation on the stance and

---

42 "The Daughter of *Herodias*" (268).

43 "Nosco virum, quem diuini comitantur odores, / Et cui sidereum splendet in ore decus" (514; CSELii 244-245).

44 The full metaphor in Vaughan's poem, describing Isaac's soul's spiritually fertile and transforming ascent, runs for sixteen lines (ll. 47-62).

rhetoric of Vaughan's 1654 Preface to *Silex Scintillans*. Vaughan's turn to
Paulinus in mid-career showed literary as well as spiritual discernment and
sensitivity: it is no surprise that he was attracted by Paulinus's remarkably hale
and good-humored rejection of the temporizing late-Roman worldliness of
Ausonius; and at his best, Paulinus "expresses his strong feelings with tact and
charm and his ideas with restraint and simplicity."[45]

To summarize, I would contend on the basis of the influences detected
above that Henry Vaughan's reading in St. Paulinus proved a catalyst for his
new converted poetic vision. Poets Vaughan had formerly known but not
particularly lionized, including George Herbert and St. Paulinus, now became
part of a new sacred poetic lineage reaching back, not through Habington,
Sidney, Ausonius, Petrarch, and Orpheus to Apollo (39), but instead through
Herbert, Paulinus, and Dionysius the Areopagite to Hierotheus. Much of what
modern readers perceive as Vaughan's transformation of Herbert's texts was
enabled by Herbert being only the most chronologically and linguistically
proximate literary ancestor – a choice that appears to make sense in the
context of Vaughan's authentic spiritual response to the loss of his younger
brother in the Civil Wars.

---

45 Green, *The Poetry of Paulinus of Nola*, p. 25.

Emiko Aida, *Little ball of fur*

LESLEY SAUNDERS

(A sequence of poems for my grandson-to-be, who was conceived by IVF)

Cell

*'Most people have never seen an actual embryo, nor seen one develop from
a fertilized egg cell. For them, embryos are largely "invisible" and imagined'.*
— Jane Maienschein

Looking-glass doors are double-sealed
against wind-swept smuts, what comes in
on newsprint, coins, shoes, gum, the skin

of strangers, dead-leaf crumb. Inside
it's another story, the one that begins
with a beginning and the just-so room

you can glimpse through the mirror-mist.
Step in. Put on the gown and mask,
the gloves and boots, your new habits:

movements slow as prayer, scrupulous
as daylight; the dropper and its sterile
disposable tip poised at the same slant

as a calligrapher's nib. Your breath
held as you make the merest inscription –
this tiny illumined initial, sans serif, legible.

Speculum

'In these final works [Helen Chadwick] created a vision of the pre-embryo's interdependency, whilst presenting it as a valued jewel . . . the pearl string of Nebula *and the cluster of* Opal *all make reference to the scientist's grading and selection of viable cell clusters, done with the naked eye in the manner of a jeweller selecting flawless gems . . . In* Nebula *the transparent beads, containing both cells and fragile dandelion heads, glimmer in the surrounding blue like the Pleiades floating in the emptiness of cosmic space.'* – Sue Hubbard

Look: is it with the telescope's
lunar eye or the microscope's
that I watch the quick of life
as it seems to swim across a sea
of light-years toward me?

Bathed in a bluish haze, a swale
of milk in the night sky, is this
the seed-pearl stargazers stared at
from their Baghdad towers,
fashioning an angelic science?

Or is it the bead of light eeling
in van Leeuwenhoek's lens,
the star of blood on the far side
of selfhood, the nova that one day
will be named for a newborn?

What crystalline hook-and-eye
fastens sky to time and its minutiae?
Or hand to heart? Was the child
I held and nursed the mother
for that unearthly, given hour?

Pipette

At the far end of a glass stem,
a moonstone: held in thin air

by its own delicate tides
and the scientist's slender gloved

fingertips it quivers, then steadies,
tentative as dew. The screen

is a sea of blue. Without spilling,
she must empty herself now

of all wishing. At her elbow,
a petri dish patient as ocean

waits with its nutrient waters
for the sipped drop, liquid jewel.

The Crystal Wombs of Katharinenthal

'Gertrude of Helfta once witnessed the immaculate womb of the glorious virgin, as transparent as the purest crystal, through which her internal organs, penetrated and filled with divinity, shone brightly . . .' – Jacqueline Jung

For most of our lives
we are self-mysterious,
the marbled walls of our flesh

windowless and massive:
we may not inspect the rooms

of the house we call home –
once in a blue moon comes
a lightening of the dark, day-break

parting the night from itself,
a *zona pellucida* at the farthest edge.

And suddenly there it is,
both visible and inward, a crystal womb
like a cup of summer rain,

like supple glass.
With what lucid technology

did the mediaeval sisters see
the coming child curled, nursing
at his mother's heart?

We are the seers of visions now,
and brimming with bliss.

In Vitro

In the earliest times when the world
was made of glass the only words were

utterly and beautiful. The evening sun
shone deep in the eyes of the singers

and the slow gift of a bird flew over
the gilded face of the congregation.

And what had been a full stop flickered
into a comma, a pause or leap between

what went before and what was to come,
its breath was a feather of sky lulling

the year from seed to leaf to field, while
fish flicked their tails in the green-glass sea.

RICHARD BERENGARTEN

From *Notness*

The Doubling

The doubling of a thing into a sign
and back again, along the two-way strings
perception and phenomena entwine
constitutes thinghood. Each thing, rippling rings
outward through spacetime, gets remade, refurled,
(recurled, returned, retwirled,) on circumstance,
to *in*form (*re*form) *this*. And so this world
whirls (whorls) things in proliferating dance.
Things' thinghoods replicate complexities
whose echoes underpin the miracle
this *here-now* is – recurring geometries
of bounty (fulness, plenty, overspill) –
excessive, but just so, in all that is –
a Star of David in a daffodil.

Home

Shekhinah

Gift to my heart, my soul's hostess and home,
interior, bless'd before time ever was,
before *wherefores* and *whys*, before *because*,
temple of skies with starred or clouded dome;
treasure so quickly gone I cannot wait
when loss sets in with its cold stony grin
and occupies all space that's left within –
useless I weep, *Gone, gone*, and weep too late
for absence to scry miserable fate.
Yet home is this and you whatever this
in presence proffers to my innerness –
you guest, you gust of wind, you swinging gate –
with you and this now how could I not still
be sure that I belonged in miracle?

Once, twice . . .

Considering this onceness, its uniqueness,
I think it, as eternity condensed
into one point, unscathed, uninfluenced
by any *else*, having no hole or weakness.
Hence *now* is what holds *nothing*, being *isness*
itself – in pure perfection – made, unmade
only to bloom – not bud, grow, wither, fade,
and with no other state, shape, role or business.
Yet *now* repeats, repeats – and every one
of all its unfurled, pleated nothingnesses
(out of last *notness*, past, mere dream, gone, done)
melts, merges, in the next *now* it addresses.
If now's unique, twiceness, its forfeiture
yields it to *after* through and from *before*.

A Resonance

My other came. His glance did not offend.
He stood between this building and a ground
that faded into mist at its far end.
No bird in branches made a single sound.
'This is my other and my brother,' said
a voice that spawned from nowhere in my head,
'but which one breathes on this side, and which dead,
is quite uncertain here, despite the dread
that occupies you each in double presence.'
This happened in (across) two sets of eyes
through quiet, in a kind of reticence.
The hills said nothing in their paradise
but echoed, chiming, in a resonance
as fast as light, past shock, past (passed) surprise.

Text and Intertext

This moment is perfection, paradise.
Its fulness could not be the more complete.
Then comes the next and grips it like a vice,
squeezing it out at each new moment's feet.
Each passes being opened. None will last,
no sooner aired, dispersed in airiness.
Not that each moment 'betters' each one past,
disgorged, exhausted, spent in weariness;
nor that each one's not infinitely vast –
to each its *thisness here*, its veryness.
And so it goes: next, next, and afternext,
each cracking each no sooner than begun.
As *Midrashim* illuminate a text
each heaven breaks, renews, each previous one.

Dot

Illuminated by concentric rings
blazing, pulsating radiance, this mere dot
of consciousness, this point that sobs and sings
is governed by what is. There's not a jot
this universe consists of – quanta, strings –
apparent among images that things
cast into moving patterns – that is not
keyed to this context, mesh, maze, fabric, plot
of undulations, spirals, mirrorings.
Without co-ordinates of space and time
and, who knows, many more dimensions still,
each repetition, variation, chime
that forms this moment's common miracle
would bear scant pressure, weight, flow, stress or rhyme
or let this empty purse of *notness* fill.

SAM ADAMS

21 September, 7.15 am

Sky yellow, silver barred, clouds laid
in impasto streaks along horizon
southwards:
jumped up on patio where bay tree
grows fox of a sudden made free
of garden – orange, black-tipped ears,
lifting delicately paws, one and one
and one, and one, brushing patio's
heaps of fallen leaves.

Fox looked slowly up
and down, and sat in rustling
litter of leaves and hazel nuts and
broken shells, sat breaking
nuts in snarling teeth and chewing,
ears black-tipped twitch-twitching,
looked up
and down, cracking nuts, chew-chewing,
freeholder fox of a morning yellow,
barred silver, clouds impasto rose
along horizon south.

25/26 September

What creature's call is that – a barking
mew, or mewing bark – some hybrid of
seagull and bereft small dog,
chimerical?
Pressed flat to a withy branch,
tail dramatically furled,
a squirrel howls from the edges
of an unknown world.

What daft charade is this, what
crazy pantomime? Squirrel
interring hazel nuts pursued
by magpie that has it by the tail,
leaning back and holding
as squirrel pulls the other way.

And this morning's
squirrel on the patio's lost
a good half of its bushy train.
It climbs lilac tree, begins
its barking serenade – to a chorus
of magpie laughter.

What is all this to do? A land
dispute? Or species tug of war,
in which mammal is defeated
by feathered dinosaur?

30 May

Blue bubble over, sun
rising still on blue eye
below, still clarity streaked
with light – and movement:
glazed as oil, imperceptible
to silt even goldfish stir, pale
coiling sinuosity under glass.

Free of water, and
glistening still in sun
on stone, stout thread of green
trickle spills into
begonia's cabbage patch.

Screams then from untrimmed
grass below tilted fence:
flat, long mouth drawing
in puffed frog, puffed eyes
pounding, screaming still,
sky and sun unblinking.

CLARE CROSSMAN

from *Peloponnese*

1. *Stefani**

This May I am returning home to my village,
away from the petrol and dust of the city.
Born from rain and the January dark,
the wildflowers seem to grow out
of air: chamomile, iris, oregano, daisies.
As if Zeus had scattered them all
as he passed. I will braid them to circles;
hang them at my door. Bind a sheaf
with an ear of wheat for Demeter.

We were always sailors, fish of the river,
voyaging out from green waters
into the Aegean, searching for ivory,
obsidian, amber and glass.
When invaders came we had the mountains,
partisan, bare. We lived in the forests
waited high up with the goats, for their passing.

The world is an eye that can turn blue.
I prefer a white horse, this yard full of shade,
time to sit at the table with friends.
The sea at my door.
There are too many islands to take.
While I am here it is right I think,
to believe in light and flowers.

Greek Spring Festival, May 1st

June at Dowcra's Manor

'all mornings are mysteries'

The courtyard is a snatch of a far country.
The paving stones absorb heat from the sun,
water lilts of the sea and a quenched thirst.

Here is for fig and lavender to grow.
And rosemary its rust taste, strong as honey.
There might be lemons or a jasmine covered wall.

Enclosed, we sit here in summer pretending
we are high in the mountains, tin bells of goats
at the edge of hearing, in the clear air.

The lily pollen on my hands soaks a rain charm.
Slowly the grasses dry and the heads of artichokes
burn among the green.

Swallows arrive with high calls, and indigo wings.
In their returning they dart between doors,
sit high in the eaves, studding the day.
This is one way to bring the distance home.

I sit on this terrace, half awake, sun behind my eyes.
In the day light's unravelling,
what language should I speak?

ALEX BARR

Ash

A sestina

I'm spreading ash from the fire
on the yard, in a snaking pattern
from a carrier bag onto compacted stones.
It's lucky there's no wind.
The black sky is clear, the stars perfect,
the Plough a signal, Jupiter a torch.

I'm spreading ash in the beam of a torch.
The year is dying. We sit before the fire
consoling ourselves that nothing is ever perfect.
Weeping and laughter weave a pattern.
Shrivelled leaves are herded by the wind
into the bed of the stream among the stones.

Rain will bed down the ash between the stones
of the yard. I've thrown away the torch
as useless, and now I'm listening to the wind
in the chimney stirring the embers of the fire.
Nights and days make a syncopated pattern
that in hindsight may seem perfect.

Parts of the dying year *were* almost perfect.
Children gathered veined and mottled stones
to arrange on the garden steps in a pattern
they understood. At night we used a torch
to hunt for slugs and mushrooms. The fire
wasn't needed. We flew kites in a gentle wind.

Remember all that, remember! While the wind
tears at the trees and sings a perfect
anthem of solitude. Stoke up the fire,
carry the ash to spread among the stones,
remember to buy a more reliable torch,
gaze at the heavens's undeciphered pattern.

Our lives are embedded in the endless pattern
of generations borne along by the wind
of Time. If we are bearers of the torch
of hope and wisdom, we are no less perfect
than those who raised the rings of standing stones,
measured the lunar months, and discovered fire.

Ash from our stove will make a perfect
bed for our footsteps there among the stones
we tread to search for logs to stoke the fire.

JOHN KILLICK

Remembering James Leggatt (1896-1993)

There were times when I thought you might
have made that century for the village team:
standing there blinking in the evening light,

still upstanding at the crease, still proud
of all those decades of country devotion,
before eventually entering the pavilion.

But it wasn't to be: you looked away,
your attention held for a moment
by the ducks straddling the stream;

or, in that room where you went
for lessons, by the sound of the violin
riding the water's delirium;

or by the sight of dear Marjorie, leaving
the village store wearing that print dress
which evermore would catch at the breath.

Whichever it was, it seems you were
caught out, not by inattention
but a sudden sense of the undersong.

PATRICK BOND

Shaving by Candlelight

Not that I must, but only wish it so: free of glare
I track the skin's labile lift and fold by lustre,
by glow of the small source, the flame in the mirror;

and the cutting edge by its singular clicks and rasps,
the fine sweep and sting of steel, its mayhem
by absence, achieved silence, a posthumous caress.

The press of hot flannel releases my long stare. Eyes shut,
I trace the thrusts and hollows of facial bones: eye-sockets,
jaw-line, cheek ridge; brace the cooling flesh for what must be so.

ANNE CLUYSENAAR

That donkey, she was my freedom.
Tap of her unshod hooves
till she turned off on the track.

Green grass, white hedges and
(as I remember it now)
celandines, lords and ladies,

with winding short perspectives
beyond which, mystery –
the well-known, always new.

We'd seek the circular bed
of a gypsy fire – one, in sight
for me now as I feel her knees

buckle and just have time
to slide away as she rolls,
furring us both in ash.

The joy then of riding home
anointed with distance, the cling
of directions not yet tried.

Winding rather than straight
my liking still, with no end
clearly in sight, no chance

of merely turning for home,
the bonfires mine, the travel
through time but in mind too.

Years are forcing a freedom
I didn't need then. Not only
the path discovered, but changing

as I ride the hooves of a poem.

I hope it still happens, as then
when fishing-boats, nosing the harbour,
waited for blessing. A crowd

lined the shore. And at shoulder height
a Virgin was winding her way
where, for a time, no traffic

other than metaphor passed.
She has, from earliest days,
promised a chance for change.

At first, less of a girl,
breasts heavy and hips broad,
bare of that heavenly blue,

tiny enough to be carried
in just one hand wherever
a man or woman might go.

Now, it's the unforeseeable
we think of: cells in the womb
fusing to make new chances.

That time – the ocean ablaze
under its boats, the shore
edged by both old and young,

psalms beyond sight approaching
now loud, now dim through the streets –
survives in me still to this day.

The blessing we waited for
I no longer hear, but I do
see a gesture seeding the deep,

a drop or two blessed by hope.

Why click on *Fontaine de Vaucluse*?
Didn't I trust the spring
in my head, pulsing dark and clear?

To stand, as a girl, where he stood
at the start of a great river,
source of so many thoughts,

where he saw or imagined love
resting naked there in the flow,
shaded by a gentle branch!

To stand there then was not
as it would be now. I'd be moved
that he sought, though years had passed,

a trace of her feet in the grass,
found that her eyes had touched
with brightness all his might see.

'More certainty would be loss',
a courageous thought that came
as language explored his heart.

They found him dead, at long last,
his head laid down on the page,
a pen still clasped in his hand.

On the net, this well-smoothed path,
grassless, treeless, this pool
too big, too sunny, too clear,

is not what I've had in mind
all these years, as my Helicon:
stony, tree-hung, a pulse –

half hidden – wafting the grass.

Martyred Signs: Robert Southwell's religious use of metaphor

NOAM REISNER

On February 20th, 1595, Robert Southwell, Jesuit priest and poet, was brought before the Queen's Bench for trial under the Elizabethan act against Jesuits and Seminarists of 1585. As Southwell waited for the inevitable verdict of treason and the grim sentencing that was sure to follow, he was asked of his age and is reported to have stated that he 'was near about the age of our Saviour' when he was crucified. When Richard Topcliff, the priest-hunter who arrested Southwell, denounced him for his pride in making such a blasphemous comparison, Southwell is said to have rejoined that he considered himself 'a humble worm created by Christ'.[1] The agonized identification of the contrite Christian sinner with the crucified Christ is a commonplace of early modern devotional poetry on both sides of the Reformation divide, where the potential blasphemy of the identification is usually balanced by immediate qualifications of the sinner's unworthiness of Christ's blood. However, in recalling this metaphoric image at that moment, Southwell was consciously drawing on the theatrical and sacer-dotal aspects of his literal role as a witness, that is, a martyr, to the suffering and sacrifice of Christ on the cross.

Knowing he had an audience whose religious sympathies may not have been as clear-cut as the legal occasion should have warranted (as already evidenced by Southwell's letter to Sir Robert Cecil, written from his confinement in the Tower on 6 April 1593)[2], Southwell was at that moment materially presenting

---

1 One of the main sources containing an account of Southwell's trial is a letter from Fr Henry Garnet to the general of the Society of Jesus in Rome, Claudio Acquaviva, dated 22 February 1595. Letter quoted in Philip Caraman, *The Other Face: Catholic Life under Elizabeth I* (London: Longmans, 1960), p. 230. See also Nancy Pollard Brown, "Robert Southwell", in *Oxford Dictionary of National Biography*.

2 The letter is at once a partial confession and a plea for clemency, banking on Cecil's sympathy, if not for a Jesuit, then for a man devoted to his family. By insisting in the letter the he only returned to England to tend to his family's spiritual needs, and not act in the Jesuit mission, Southwell was hoping to depend on the privacy of spiritual concerns otherwise allowed under Elizabethan law. Southwell was most likely hoping to draw in this case on his personal association with Robert Cecil's nephew, William Cecil, who visited Rome without his family's approval in 1585 and was rumoured (perhaps wrongly) of having converted to Catholicism. Southwell's gamble did not pay off, as Robert Cecil took no action, and later used the letter to bring Southwell to trial. See Brown, *ODNB*.

himself as an example in imitation of Christ for his disciples and fellow members of the Jesuit mission to England. The predictable sentence was handed down, and soon after Southwell was taken out to Tyburn to face the horror of being hung, drawn and quartered. As he ascended the scaffold, he crossed himself, and asked to address the crowd. On the scaffold, he prayed for the salvation of Queen and country, and asked that he might find perseverance 'unto the end of this my laste conflicte'. After years of being denied a pulpit in his outlawed ministry, he was finally able to make use of one very publicly. Contemporary accounts of the event from sympathetic fellow Catholics claim that his words moved the horrified crowd so much, that none cried 'traitor' when his severed head was presented to them.[3] Following his execution, Southwell was instantly recognized and celebrated as a martyr by the Catholic Church, and in 1970 was canonized by Pope Paul VI as a saint and one of the Forty Martyrs of England and Wales.

Robert Southwell, then, like Edmund Campion and many other Jesuit missionaries in Protestant England before and after him, was a man destined for martyrdom. As prefect of studies of the English Jesuit college in Rome, Southwell wrote in 1586 to Claudio Acquaviva, general of the society, with a request that he should be allowed to serve on the English mission: 'in the same way as Your Paternity approves of my present work among the English, so by the inspiration of God may you also approve of my service in England itself, with the highest hope of martyrdom'[4]. By May that year, Southwell began his long journey towards home and the ultimate realization of his wish for martyrdom. Largely based in London under the alias 'Cotton', and enjoying some measure of protection from Anne Howard, the countess of Arundel and Surrey, Southwell found he was an outlaw priest serving an outlawed community. He used his poems and prose sermons, circulated and copied in contraband manuscript and occasionally print as well, to administer the spiritual needs of a congregation denied a church and the open practice of its rituals.

Southwell's poems, however, not only seek to administer to an absent congregation, but also pattern out in the suffering voice of the poem's speaker a masochistic fantasy of suffering that relies on a central transubstantive metaphor in which words become metaphorical flesh in the spiritual affect of the poem, acting out the life and death of a martyred voice.[5] Posthumous print editions of Southwell's poems published in London soon after his execution, such as the *Moeniae* (1595), carefully censored elements in Southwell's manuscript poems

---

3 Brown and Caraman, ibid. See also Anne R. Sweeney, *Robert Southwell – Snow in Arcadia: Redrawing the English Lyric Landscape, 1586-95* (Manchester: Manchester University Press, 2006), pp. 260-2.

4 Quoted in Brown, *ODNB*.

5 See Sweeney, *Snow in Arcadia*, pp. 253-7, 269-86.

that came too close to suggest a narrative of martyrdom that could potentially then be read back into the life of the poet.[6] Such fears were entirely justified, not because of a casual thematic reading imposed onto the poems, but because these were readings written in and demanded of the texts themselves as part of their intense meta-poetic sacramentality. Long before Southwell actually ascended the Tyburn scaffold to undergo actual martyrdom, he had played out this moment with the intended addressees of his poems by enacting martyrdom in word, metaphor and tortured icon. His poems are textual martyrs that bear witness not only to the persecution and suffering he had to endure as an individual, but also to the martyred state of his persecuted beliefs and doctrines, which came to symbolize the height of idolatry in the eyes of its iconoclastic, Protestant enemies.

My argument is in two parts. First, I will address the nature of Southwell's sacramental poetics in general, claiming that the principal metaphoric operation of a typical Southwell poem seeks to override the metaphoric structure of poetic representation itself. In line with Roman Catholic sacramental theory about the miraculous operation that turns the signs of the Host literally into that which they signify, Southwell allows his devotional metaphors to cancel out themselves, as overt didacticism gives you to experiential sacramentalism. I will then proceed to look at how this sacramentality interacts with the uses of the first person pronoun in the poems to generate a visceral drama of martyrdom. By inserting his own priestly persona into the aforementioned process of anti-metaphoric rapture, Southwell generates a correlative experience of martyrdom that is overwhelmingly affective rather than simply thematic or declarative.

*

In an important study, Regina Schwartz has argued that what we understand today as the birth of modern secularism in the sixteenth century came about in many ways through the Reformers' relentless assault on the premise of sacramentality, where a sign was thought not only to stand in for something else otherwise absent, but to effect a reality in bridging the fallen and divine worlds.

---

6 James H. McDonald and Nancy Pollard Brown, eds., *The Poems of Robert Southwell, S. J.* (Oxford: Clarendon, 1967), p. 19. In quoting the poems of Southwell, however, I have relied on the more recent edition of Peter Davidson and Anne Sweeney, eds., *St. Robert Southwell: Collected Poems* (Manchester: Carcanet, 2007). The editions differ greatly from one another. McDonald and Brown established an authoritative text for the poems by collating printed editions with available manuscript variants. Davidson and Sweeney, however, directly transcribe the poems in their different manuscript versions, ignoring later printed editions, and faithfully reproducing the way the poems were written on the page by the different copyists. This latter way of approaching Southwell's clandestine poetic ministry is more sensible, especially if one hopes to make a cogent claim about the intended reader-response of these poems.

Sacramental poetry, argues Schwartz, 'is a poetry that signifies more than it says, that creates more than it signs, yet does so, like liturgy, through image, sound, and time, in language that takes the hearer beyond each of those elements'.[7] Although Schwartz does not discuss Southwell's poetry at all in her study, this latter model equally serves as an account of what Sweeney and others have shown was the poetic practice of Southwell's Jesuit mission.[8] For Southwell, who was fully invested in the efficaciously redemptive power of the Roman Mass, God was immanent in all human acts of signification. Unlike Protestant poets who came after him, he was untroubled by the Reformers' problematic dismantling of the structures of transcendence and efficacy underpinning the Roman Mass, which they held to be idolatrous. If, for example, Schwartz detects in the devotional poetry of John Donne a mournful lament for the shrinking away of sacramental experience,[9] in Southwell presumably such experience is celebrated and affirmed. If Southwell had any role to play then in the birth of modernity on Schwartz's terms, it was either by setting up a clear model of the sacramentality that was now to be eschewed, or by inspiring later so-called 'metaphysical' poets, especially Herbert and Crashaw, in rethinking the demands of a sacramental poetics in light of these theological upheavals.

While Schwartz's definition of what constitutes sacramental poetry in general is very suggestive, it risks oversimplifying the deep crisis traditional sacramentlists such as Southwell equally must have faced with regards to the potential efficacy of their devotional lyrics following the rupture of the Reformation. Moreover, in its very nature as mediated sacramentality, Southwell's poetry may very well have shown the way for later Roman Catholic poets, as well as High-Church English Protestants, to redefine, rather than altogether discard, the sacramental efficacy of devotional experience in light of the emerging crisis in transcendental signification. After all, we must never forget that celebrating the Mass is one thing, but to offer a persecuted congregation a poem that would metaphorically stand in for the Mass is something else entirely. In other words, Southwell's poetry attempts to renegotiate the use of metaphorical language in the context of Roman Catholic piety by testifying to its suffering when persecuted by those who would seek violently to sever sign from signified, tenor

---

7 Regina M. Schwartz, *Sacramental Poetics at the Dawn of Secularism: When God Left the World* (Stanford: Stanford University Press, 2008), p. 7.

8 Sweeney, *Snow in Arcadia*, pp. 240-2. See also more generally, Pierre Janelle, *Robert Southwell the Writer* (London: Sheed and Ward, 1935), Louis Martz, *The Poetry of Meditation: A Study in English Religious Poetry of the Seventeenth Century* (New Haven: Yale University Press, 1954, rev. 1962), Anthony Raspa, *The Emotive Image: Jesuit Poetics in the English Renaissance* (Fort Worth: Texas Christian University Press, 1983), Ceri Sullivan, *Dismembered Rhetoric: English Recusant Writing, 1580 to 1603* (London: Associated University Presses, 1995).

9 Schwartz, pp. 87-116.

from vehicle. It points to the shrinking away of divine immanence in human affairs by at once lamenting that loss and seeking to fill the resulting void with an experiential testimony of suffering in the face of such a loss. In essence, therefore, such a stance is only different in degree, not in kind, from that of poets like Donne or Herbert, who mournfully explore the consequences of such iconoclasm on their devotional art and confessional outlook.[10]

It is true of course that the Reformed Eucharistic controversy, which began with Luther's increasingly outspoken attack on Zwingli's sacramental theology, rendered the sort of iconic sacramentality developed for example by Southwell untenable for Protestant poets, but it also provided no clear alternatives. It is often remarked that the Reformation movement collapsed the distinction between an active and a contemplative religion, and substituted in its spiritual economy words for things, as opposed for allowing words to become things.[11] Luther's great hermeneutical discovery about God's 'speech-act of promise', which underpins his controversial sacramental theory of consubstantiation, entails that 'the linguistic sign is itself the reality, that it represents not an absent but a present reality'[12]. For Luther, the divine Word, or logos, establishes a relationship between man and God in a way which authorizes the words of the Word not merely to signify but to effect, not in the Catholic sense of one becoming the other, but in the sense of the one being bound and contained within the other. As Lee Palmer Wandel puts it, 'God's words [for Luther] were not to be bent to human imagination, human tradition, human sensibilities . . .

10 For the influence of Southwell on Donne, Herbert and later 'metaphysical' poets see Alison Shell, *Catholicism, Controversy and the English Literary Imagination* (Cambridge: Cambridge University Press, 1999), ch. 2. In general, several critics in the past have attempted to outline a 'sacramental' mode of poetry in Donne or Herbert that may be said to anticipate Sweeney on Southwell or Schwartz more generally on the phenomenon. See Eleanor J. McNees, *Eucharistic Poetry: The Search for Presence in the Writings of John Donne, Gerard Manley Hopkins, Dylan Thomas, and Geoffrey Hill* (Lewisburg: Bucknell University Press, 1992), Judith H. Anderson, *Words That Matter: Linguistic Perception in Renaissance English* (Stanford: Stanford University Press, 1996), Theresa M. DiPasquale, *Literature and Sacrament: The Sacred and the Secular in John Donne* (Pittsburgh: Duquesne University Press, 1999), Robert Whalen, *The Poetry of Immanence: Sacrament in Donne and Herbert* (Toronto and London: University of Toronto Press, 2002). However, Schwartz was the first explicitly to draw the implication of sacramental poetics for the emergence of secularism, which all of the above critics point to, and which indirectly enough places Southwell in this tradition as a formative precursor of Donne's and Herbert's displaced sacramentality, notwithstanding the differences in confessional outlook.

11 For some of the literary and linguistic implications of this idea see Anderson, pp. 137-165. For the general 'semantic shift' in the perception of language in the Renaissance, especially following the Reformation, see Richard Waswo, *Language and Meaning in the Renaissance* (Princeton: Princeton University Press, 1987).

12 Oswald Byer, 'Luther as an interpreter of Holy Scripture', trans. Mark Mattes, in Donald L. McKim, ed., *The Cambridge Companion to Martin Luther* (Cambridge: Cambridge University Press, 2003), 73-85, at p. 76.

For all their difficulty, their impenetrability, these words were fixed – sufficient, essential, determinative, and absolute'[13]. While this is true in a very general conceptual sense, we ought to admit the fraught nature of this paradoxical idea. The most that such a shift away from works to words can achieve is to dislocate the moment of ineffable surrender from its traditional place at the heart of the religious experience and locate it, indeterminately, outside the scriptural horizon of the Reformed Christian's religious life. However, that same ineffable, sacramental presence still hovers on that horizon, insinuating itself into the gaps between the words of the Word, putting any conceivable Protestant 'speech-act' under the tremendous strain of having to contain within it divine or sacramental 'real presence' even while precluding it.[14]

The spiritual anxiety and semiotic indeterminacy such theological confusion breeds is apparent in the emerging theories of sacramental signification current in Elizabethan England – currents which Southwell's poetic ministry sought to confound for their relentless equivocation. Most English reformers followed Calvin in seeking a compromise between Lutheran consubstantiation and Zwinglian memorialism, advocating what theologian Brian Gerrish has described as either a process of 'symbolic parallelism' or 'symbolic instrumentalism' in the sacramental ritual.[15] Instrumentalists such as High-Church luminary Bishop Lancelot Andrewes generally leaned towards Lutheran consubstantiation (via Martin Chemnitz) in advocating that sacramental symbols, while not actively becoming something else in a transubstantive sense, effectively cause what they symbolize and are efficacious in themselves in an instrumental sense.[16] Parallelists such as Elizabethan Calvinist divine William Perkins, on the other hand, refined Zwingli via Calvin and taught that there was a parallel, rather than strictly memorial, relationship between the sacramental symbols and their transcendental referents. Such parallelism was seen to be exclusively predicated on faith and to be efficacious only in assuring the elect of their Justification.

13 Lee Palmer Wandel, *The Eucharist in the Reformation: Incarnation and Liturgy* (Cambridge: Cambridge University Press, 2006), pp. 94-5.

14 For more on the overall apophatic context of these claims, see Noam Reisner, *Milton and the Ineffable* (Oxford: Oxford University Press, 2009), pp. 56-104.

15 The terms sacramental 'memorialism', 'parallelism', and 'instrumentalism' were first coined by Brian A. Gerrish in 'The Lord's Supper in the Reformed Confessions' (1966), reprinted in *The Old Protestantism and the New: Essays on the Reformation Heritage* (Edinburgh: T. & T. Clark, 1982), pp. 118-130. See also Gerrish, *Grace and Gratitude: The Eucharistic Theology of John Calvin* (Edinburgh: T. & T. Clark, 1993), p. 167, and more generally C. W. Dugmore, *The Mass and the English Reformers* (London: McMillan, 1958), and B. D. Spinks, *Sacraments, Ceremonies and the Stuart Divines: Sacramental Theology and Liturgy in England and Scotland 1603-1662* (Aldershot: Ashgate, 2002).

16 For the sacramental aspirations of Andrewes's pulpit prose see Noam Reisner, 'Textual Sacraments: Capturing the Numinous in the Sermons of Lancelot Andrewes', *Renaissance Studies* 21: 5 (2007), 662-78.

In his Elizabethan bestseller, *The Golden Chaine*, Perkins labels such parallelism as 'the sacramental relation' and in the process provides one of the most lucid expositions of this pervasive Reformed doctrine, which clearly denies both Lutheran consubstantiation and the modified theories of instrumentalism:

> The sacramentall union. I. Is not naturall according to place: for there is no mutation of the signe into the thing signed, neither is the thing signed, either included in, or fastned upon the signe. But II. It is respective, because there is a certaine agreement and proportion of the externall things with the internall, and of the actions of one with the actions of the other: whereby it commeth to passe, that the signes, as it were certaine visible words incurring into the externall senses, doe by a certain proportionable resemblance draw a Christian minde to the consideration of things signified, and to be applyed. This mutuall, as I may say, sacramentall relation, is the cause of so many figurative speeches and Metonymies which are used: as when one thing in the Sacrament is put for another.[17]

It should be noted that when Perkins says that the sacramental relation as established in Christ's institution of the Lord's Supper results in 'figurative speeches', his tone is one of regret. For Perkins, there is something spiritually instructive but also dangerous about the sacramental union as he sees it, where the mutable world of perishable symbols and the immutable world of God's grace are imagined as two parallel lines that can never meet, but which nevertheless imperfectly mirror one another. Such an analogical relationship is spiritually rewarding because it allows the Christian mind, reflecting inwardly on its state of grace, to see the process of justification mirrored in 'external sensible' objects and rituals. At the same time, it is also a dangerous process because it can potentially distract the naturally infirm Christian mind, vitiated by sin, to dwell too much on the symbols themselves rather than on the thing symbolized. For this reason, the Lord's Supper was always inferior and subordinate to preaching in evangelical practice, where the operative word is that of 'sealing'. The visible, commemorative trappings of the Lord's Supper give the contrite Communicant assurance of 'justification' only *if* the spiritual sacramental relation is upheld and is allowed to seal the elect person in grace, and it can *only* be upheld by hearing the Word of God preached, both before and after the ritual itself.

---

17 William Perkins, *The Works of that Famous and Worthy Minister of Christ . . . William Perkins*. 3 vols., (London: 1626-35), vol. 1, p. 72.

Against this background of theological unrest, Southwell's reaffirmation and celebration of Roman Catholic orthodoxy is not merely defensive, but actively adversarial. Like many other Tridentine theologians, Southwell grasped the inherent paradox in the Reformer's struggle with ineffability in their devotional practices and sought to confront it on its own terms. The orthodox Roman Catholic Eucharistic position, made official by a decretal of Pope Innocent III in 1215 and continually developed theologically since then from Aquinas to Scotus, up to the formal pronouncements issuing from the Council of Trent, maintains that during the miracle of transubstantiation the substance of the Host radically and miraculously changes into the body of Christ *per modum substantiae*, while the Host's accidents, such as taste, texture and colour, remain unchanged *in loco*. Only God, the transcendental author of creation, may bend his own universal laws (which Aristotle was believed to have inspirationally expounded) and change the substance of a thing without altering its accidents. For Roman Catholics, therefore, Jesus' institution of the Lord's Supper with the words, to quote the AV's Matthew 26:26, 'take, eat, this *is* my body' (*hoc est enim corpus meum*), presupposes a metaphorical miracle where the bread and wine of the sacrament literally become in a mystical sense a substantive or essential body and blood.

Southwell evidently grasped that the Protestant instrumentalist compromise – and even Perkin's more stridently reformed parallelist stance – differed finally from the orthodox understanding of sacred metaphorical function by nuanced degrees, not in fundamental principles. The question always returns to the function of metaphor in the rituals of the church. However, while the Reformed rejection of transubstantiation was clear enough in abstract theological terms, the semiotic implications of such a rejection for the metaphorical nature of religious ritual were not. Ironically, in seeking to replace the Host with poetry, Southwell himself was participating in the same struggle for sacramental redefinition, except of course that as he saw it, he was driven to such desperate, and therefore creative, measures by his persecutor's errors to which his own sacramental poetry stood as righteous testimony. The transubstantive belief in the incarnational power of words was therefore central to Southwell's clandestine ministry in its enactment of an ongoing martyrdom that is grasped by its intended readers not didactically or symbolically, but sacramentally, as a shared numinous experience centred on a sacred object, in this case the poem on the page. Transporting into words the baroque images of Italian religious painting, and the intense sacramentalism and performative energies of High Roman Mass and Latin liturgy, Southwell crafted poems that could communicate, indeed stand in for, the otherwise ineffable workings of ecstatic religious ritual, and what is known in sacramental theology as the elusive promise of 'real presence'.

For Southwell, however, the transubstantive conceit precisely depends on a radical form of literalisation, where the metaphorical structure of substitution implied in the Gospel words is replaced, as a matter of faith, with the operation of a miracle that finally cancels out the metaphorical dimension of language itself. Southwell's poetry points to the radically ineffable, sacred presence that attends the solemn moment of the Host's physical consumption: the Eucharistic bread and wine are not metaphors, but miraculously transformed sacral objects.

The conceptual problem facing Southwell then in coming to write efficacious sacramental poetry should be evident: whatever else a poem is, it cannot stand in for the Eucharistic Host, except by metaphorical enactment of the related experience, which in turn depends on the final cancelling out of that same metaphorical dimension of the language used. In this regard, Southwell's poetry is intentionally rather than incidentally paradoxical. Much of Southwell's sacral poetry tends towards the extreme effusion of paradox where the poem offers itself as a consecrated Host by precisely blurring the metaphorical correspondences between tenors and their vehicles. 'Real presence' thus becomes available to the reader lyrically through a process of counter-intuitive reading which replaces didactic comprehension with a deliberate confounding of the rational instinct to grasp sense and meaning as 'something understood' (to employ the famous line by Herbert),[18] beyond language and signification.

This process almost always begins in a Southwell poem with an intense iconographic focus on discrete objects: a burning babe, the virigin's breasts, or face, or hands, the groaning cross, the crown of thorns, Christ's wounds, streaming blood, streaming tears, the altar of the mass, etc. These objects, often making up an elaborate ekphrastic description, function as the sacral focal point of Southwell's piety, accruing in the process of near obsessive verbal adoration something like real sacramental presence, as language breaks down and gives way to unspeakable rapture. The affective intensity of the emerging poetry extends from a literarily enacted sacramental process, where the more intense the lyrical meditation on a single metaphorical correspondence between objects becomes, so the metaphorical correspondence itself weakens, leaving the reader with a collection of flattened images on the one hand, and a deep sense of spiritual rapture on the other. This movement is nowhere better illustrated than in Southwell's famous vision of 'The burning babe' (as transcribed by Davidson and Sweeney from the Waldgrave Manuscript):

> As I in hoary Winters night stoode shyveringe in the snowe
> Surpris'd I was with sodayne heat, which made my hart to glowe

---

18 George Herbert, 'Prayer I', line 14.

And lifting upp a fearefull eye to vewe what fire was nere
A pretty babe all burninge bright did in the ayre appeare
Who scorched with excessive heate such floodes of teares did shedd
As though his floodes should quench his flames, which with his
    teares were fedd
Alas quoth he but newly borne in fiery heates I frye
Yet none approach to warme their hartes or feele my fire but I
My faultles brest the furnace is the fuell woundinge thornes
Love is the fire and sighs the smoke the ashes shame and scornes
The fewell Justice layeth on and Mercy blowes the coales
The metall in this furnace wrought are mens defiled soules
For which as nowe on fire I am to worke them to their good
So will I melt into a bath to washe them in my bloode.
With this he vanisht out of sight and swiftly shronke awaye
And straight I called unto mynde, that it was Christmas daye.

The iconic image of a babe floating in mid air, alight with flame, moves away from the tactile concreteness of a religious image to the calm certainties of Christian salvation through a process of speech and paradox. As the babe speaks to the poet, rapt in his vision, the force of religious paradox depends initially on sustaining the metaphorical construction of x is y. This construction, however, is increasingly undermined not just by the syntactical form of the poem, but also in the poem's manuscript layout reproduced above. There are no stanza breaks, and hardly any punctuation marks to dictate syntactical rhythms – only a list of nouns and their adjectives linked across the page by the copula 'is', where the analogical distinction between tenor and vehicle is transformed through the theological conceit of a literalized metaphor into a transcendental *mixed* metaphor. This poetic sacramental ritual is enacted by the burning babe itself who speaks in a string of metaphors: 'My faultles brest' is a 'furnace', which in turn becomes the 'fuel' of wounding thorns, but also of 'Love', which Love in turn reverts back to fire again, but a fire which is now implicated metaphorically also with 'sighs', which are in turn 'the smoke the ashes shame and scorns'. The sense of a mixed metaphor growing exponentially by accumulating vehicles creates an arch-metaphor which captures something of the *feeling* of sacramental rapture itself, where the more expansive the language becomes, the more intense the sacral silence generated by its metaphorical indeterminacy.

The intensity of numinous religious feeling thus depends here and elsewhere in Southwell's poetry on a rhetorical strategy that uses self-annihilating metaphors to finally override, as in the actual sacramental ritual of the Mass, the metaphorical structure underpinning signification. Appropriately, therefore, once the metaphorical coherence of the poem paradoxically and gradually shrinks away together with the vanishing vision of the burning babe, we are left finally only with a moment of distilled spiritual clarity about the promise of salvation on Christmas day: 'With this he vanisht out of sight and swiftly shronke awaye / And straight I called unto mynde, that it was Christmas daye'. However, the iconic surface of the poem, with its babe suspended in mid air, wreathed in flame, smoke and tears, continues to command our visual and affective attention throughout, so that as the metaphorical links dissolve into an ever shrinking, ever intensifying moment of rapture, the sense of the miraculous attached to the imagery correspondingly increases.

'The burning babe' is admittedly not a typical poem, even for Southwell. As Sweeney points out, 'it is not a hymn, a parody, a moral, a complaint, a reproof, a sermon . . . [and] is not even a poeticised spiritual exercise in the style of [Southwell's] longer work'.[19] Perhaps it is best simply to characterize it as a visionary meditation. Either way, it is evident that the poem is not meant to communicate a didactic homiletic message as such, but to communicate an intense religious experience that carries with it profound spiritual and religious implications for readers who would share Southwell's piety. So while not generically typical, 'The burning babe' is nevertheless instructive of Southwell's overall poetic strategy.

Indeed, even when Southwell aims in his poetry to be overtly didactic, his strategy remains fundamentally experiential and sacramental. The didacticism of the overall homiletic message of a given poem often depends for its impact on an affective demonstration of the religious feeling that ought to attach itself to the underlying doctrine. Such is the case, for example, in the overtly theological but also intensely sacramental poem, 'Of the Blessed sacrament of the Aulter', which can be read not only as a statement of religious belief about Christ's real presence in the Eucharistic Host, but also as a statement about the claims of spiritual truth Southwell wishes to attach to the body of the poem as well, for example in the third stanza (Waldegrave Manuscript):

> They sawe they harde they felt him sitting nere
> Unseene unfelt unhard they him receiv'd
> No diverse thinge though divers it appeare
> Though sences faile, yet faith is not deceiv'd
> And if the wonder of the worke be newe
> Believe the worke because his worde is trewe. (lines 13-18)

Southwell's poetic truth is always to be found, as this stanza suggests and 'The burning babe' demonstrates, in the religious, ineffable motions between hearing

---

19 Sweeney, *Snow in Arcadia*, p. 280.

and unhearing, seeing and unseeing. There, in the midst of sacramental rapture, is discovered the authority of Southwell's persona, the poet-priest conducting a textual Mass on our behalf. Southwell's craft of devotional poetry emerges here as a kind of miraculous 'worke', the sacramental efficacy of which the reader must believe, for 'faith is not deceiv'd' even when it is confronted by the superficial diversity of form: 'No diverse thinge though divers it appeare'. As a devoted Catholic, words for Southwell always amount to 'worke', where spiritual truth is a function of the sacramental process which sees words actively become the sacral objects they describe at the moment of imagined literary consumption. As Southwell goes on to say in the seventh stanza of the poem, 'Here', in the sacramental poem standing in for the Host, 'to delight the witt trewe wisdom is . . . And if to all all this it do not bringe / The fault is in the men not in the thinge'. The use here of the figure of *epizeuxis* (the repetition of the same word in a single sentence with no other words or connectives between then) creates a dramatic effect that far exceeds mere 'wit'. The first 'all' is the transcendental 'all' of Neo-Platonic Christianity, the 'pan' that is God in his other totality, whereas the second 'all' is the mere 'all' of the poem in its total sacramental efficacy as it rises to become more than the sum of its parts. As the reader trips over this line, the sense of a mystery requiring a leap of faith increases. The result is a conditional clause: if the poem in its totality fails to bring the reader to the totality of God's immanence then the fault is not in the sacral object, i.e. the poem, but in the reader.

As images and metaphors thus break down and distil into intense sacramental *aporia*, what stands out in any given Southwell poem is the powerful personal presence of the speaking poet, the 'I' that narrates and is also the actor of the unfolding spiritual drama. If we return to 'The burning babe', for example, the speaker who opens the poem from the point of view of the contrite sinner revealingly switches in the seventh line to the 'I' of the burning babe itself. Suddenly it is the baby Christ who speaks within the vision directly to the reader about his agony which extends from the trappings of the anticipated passion and crucifixion, to the worse agony of humanity's indifference to his suffering. Southwell could not have been unaware that the Greek noun *martyria*, otherwise rendered in Latin as *testatio*, did not only denote 'testimony' or 'evidence given in testimony', but was also a figure of speech in the art of rhetoric. To quote the definition of Henry Peacham's, *The Garden of Eloquence* (1593), *martyria* is a figure by which 'the Orator or Speaker confirmeth some thing by his owne experience'.[20] The example of the burning babe's suffering, testifying, or acting as a martyr, to his agony, functions as spiritual background to poet-speaker's confession of unworthiness. As we are

---

20 Henry Peacham, *The Garden of Eloquence* (London, 1593), p. 85.

drawn into the conceit of a limitless interior of mystical visions and feelings of contrition, the speaker uses the confessional trope at the heart of the poem's sacramental intensity to point finally to the liturgical calendar that regulates such fellow Christian feelings in the healing embrace of community. But we can tell straight away that Southwell's is a persecuted, invisible community. While many of England's Protestants rest too easily in the happy, regenerative qualities of the yuletide season, Southwell's priestly persona urges the day's solemnities, collapsing the incarnational promise with the fruition of Christ's sacrifice on the cross. He does so by drawing on his own persecuted experience, where, at one with the denied Christ of Roman Catholic piety, he can say, 'none approach to warme their hartes or feele *my* fire' (my emphasis).

The two processes in Southwell's poetry, the mimetic transubstantiation of metaphors on the one hand, and the projection of a suffering self in metaphoric substitution with the suffering Christ on the other, become then a unified process of enacted and dramatized martyrdom. Southwell achieves this by at once breaking down the form of conventional sense-making lyric structures, and holding out the speaker's agony as the affective principle around which the sacramental thrust of the poem rearranges itself on the page. One of the most striking examples of this practice is Southwell's lyric on 'Christs bloody sweate', as transcribed by Sweeny and Davidson from the Waldegrave Manuscript:

> Fatt soyle, full springe, sweete olive, grape of blisse
> That yeldes, that streames, that powres, that dost distil
> Untild, undrawne, unstampde, untouchd of presse
> Deare fruit, cleare brooks, fayre oyle, sweete wine at will
> Thus Christ unforc'd preventes in shedding bloode
> The whippes the thornes the nailes the speare and roode.
>
> He Pelicans he Phenix fate doth prove
> Whome flames consume whom streames enforce to die
> How burneth bloud howe bleedeth burning love
> Can one in flame and streame both bathe and frye
> How coulde he joyne a Phenix fyerye paynes
> In faynting pelicans still bleeding vaynes
>
> Elias once to prove gods soveraigne powre
> By praire procur'd a fier of wondrous force
> That blood and wood and water did devoure
> Yea stones and dust beyonde all natures course
> Such fire is love that fedd with gory bloode
> Doth burne no lesse then in the dryest woode

O sacred Fire come shewe thy force on me
That sacrifice to Christe I maye retorne
If withered wood for fuell fittest bee
If stones and dust yf fleshe and bloode will burne
I withered am and stonye to all good.
A sacke of dust a masse of fleshe and bloode.

As with 'The burning babe' and many other poems like these, Southwell begins the poem with an intensely sacramental word-play, in this case of a six line acrostic known in the Latin rhetorical tradition as *versus rapportatus*: a block of verses that can be read horizontally or vertically, backwards or forwards, without altering their sense, or, in this case, without altering the central iconic image of Christ's sweat and blood on the cross. These lines do not merely describe the blood of Christ pouring down his body, but sacralise its distilled drops as the efficacious liquid of the Eucharist that can flow either up or down, or from side to side in defiance of gravity, as it were. It is not merely earthly liquid that obeys the laws of literal sense-making, but a metaphor of distilled grace that is at once a 'Deare fruit', 'cleare brooks', 'fayre oyle', and 'sweete wine' that has been either 'Untild' or 'undrawne', or 'unstampde', or 'untouched of presse', from whatever vehicle Southwell may whish to ascribe to the tenor that is the body of Christ.

The operative grammatical unit here is the preposition 'un', which of course denies that any actual human action or process has taken place. If the blood streams, it is un-drawne, if it yields dear fruit, it is fruit that has grown from fat soil that is un-tild, etc., and this remains the same no matter in which combination one reads the list of verbs, nouns and adjectives that make up the verse. As with 'The burning babe', the words collapse around the profoundly ineffable image of Christ bleeding on the cross, simultaneously filling the reader's mind with a range of possible metaphorical vehicles with which to make sense of the image, but then immediately denying any such semiotic comfort. The acrostic concludes rather with a preachy admonition that holds up the impossible miracle of the first four lines' sacramental play as an exemplum for how a perfect man like Christ was 'thus' able to withstand the implements of his torture. Since the blood he shed flowed freely because he wished it to, and not because of any actual injury done to him, his suffering remains not that of a victim, but of a saviour who releases others from their otherwise flesh-bound sufferings.

The next stanza then turns to emblem and paradox to amplify the first stanza's sacramental energy. The impossibility of Christ's passion is transferred to its religious moral: that Christ would choose to die for the sins of humanity out of his love. Such extreme forms of saving love are so apposite to fallen human nature that their force can only be felt in Southwell's imagination, metaphorically, as intense burning, but then how can fire be reconciled with the liquid flowing of Christ's blood? Holding up the emblematic images of the Pelican and the Phoenix, of blood-drawing and regenerative burning, as prefiguring this paradoxical meditation, Southwell thus enhances the spiritual stakes attached to the sacramental dance of words with which he began. By tying the emblematic, quasi-allegorical images of the Phoenix and the Pelican to the intensity of paradox generates by the opening stanza, the poem moves away from a mere speculative mediation of the paradox to its affective demonstration.

At this point, however, the poem takes its most radical turn, and this is indicated not only in the text itself, but also in its subsequent reception and printing history. 'Christs bloody sweat' first appeared in print in an anonymous volume of Southwell's works, the *Moeniae*, published soon after Southwell's martyrdom in 1595. This edition, however, was heavily edited to avoid any overt Roman Catholic references and therefore possible penalties to its publisher. In the original printed version of the poem, the last two stanzas were omitted, as Sweeney conjectures, because they came 'unsafely close to contemporary martyrdoms' of Southwell himself and other Jesuit priests and seminarists.[21] But why? Clearly the poem is about self-sacrifice and martyrdom. In the last two stanzas, omitted in the *Moeniae*, Southwell creates a triangular typology that links Elijah's sacrificial fire with the suffering Jesus on the cross, and finally the speaker himself who seeks to imitate in embodied words the selfless love that would allow him to realize a Christ-like sacrifice: 'That sacrifice to Christe I maye retorne'. Indeed, as Sweeney argues, this last move clinches the poem's explicit case 'for personal commitment to the Christian principle of self-sacrifice'[22] through an intense acrostic meditation on the need for the individual sinner to merit Christ's love by burning away, as it were, the encumbrance of sinful flesh and blood that makes him precisely unworthy.

However, the last two stanzas of the poem were not shocking because their effect was merely thematic – that is, because of what they overtly show themselves to be about – but because their effect is felt as the dramatic climax of the enacted martyrdom precisely sacralised in the opening two stanzas. I suspect the editor of the *Moeniae* felt that the poem could go no further because the speaker's intense plea to stand in for the brittle wood and stone of Elijah's offering about to be burnt by divine fire, extends from the literalized sacramentalism of the opening acrostic with such dramatic immediacy that any reader

---

21 Sweeney, *Snow in Arcadia*, p. 253; See also F. W. Brownlow, *Robert Southwell* (New York: Simon & Schuster, 1996), p. 114.

22 Sweeney, ibid.

reading this poem after 1595 could have potentially found themselves reliving the acute spiritual conflict of Southwell's actual martyrdom. This is not a simple case of teleologically reading Southwell's martyrdom back into his poetry, but of the poetry consciously and forcefully demanding such readings. Southwell in this and many other poems like it is not merely reflecting upon his own death, or declaring a future intent, but rather acting out martyrdom sacramentally as a shared textual mystery. Many devotional poems in the early modern period, both Catholic and Protestant, introduce a suffering self who agonizes over his or her individual worthiness of Christ's sacrifice, but few offer such a visceral drama of suffering and of bearing witness to that suffering, that is, of enacted martyrdom, as Southwell's outlawed and silenced words.

Emiko Aida, *Linked*

ALISON BRACKENBURY

The North

Bears had been known to lick his test gear, or
a cub would fell it, with one yellowed paw.
The boat each day found him a new ice mass.
Careful as child, he sank his first, small tracks,
filled up his sheet with figures. In the slack
of noon, sea nosed around its bergs. Too wide.
He counted hours, until his boat bobbed back.

He listed every name for stars of ice,
each quiet explosion, cracks spread to crevasse.
He monitored each gap. He felt no fear,
yet caught, like sailors once, a breath of flowers,
tapped in his journal, 'We should not be here.'

Keats in Hampstead

Your couplets would come easy by the ponds
where new blue algae blooms all summer long.
You lived here for two years. And did the sun
beat, without mercy, upon everyone,
on ostlers like your father, whose horse spun,
flung him to dark; your teacher's kindly son,
who lent you Homer in one scented night
when you stayed up to read, sat down to write?
Your passions throb our heads, but not your world
of saws and joints, of blood spat, wounds unhealed.

I write to you from guilt, since I did not
complete your last home's tour; my head swam hot.
I caught the plum-red flash, your mother's ring
you slipped on a girl's finger at nineteen,
which never left it. But you did, of course,
since TB swerved at you, the bolting horse.
I could not hear you under solid eaves,
perhaps outside, amongst the huge lime leaves
which muttered thunder. Here the ponds lie still.
Like bees, eight gold-ticked ducklings whirl and mill.
'Terrible mother! She'll be left with none,'
Bread-Woman says, who flings crumbs to each one.

Should the old dog have plunged across pond's scum?
Coughs mask each liquid furrow he has swum.
You could have drunk heron's hunched quiet, the coot's
soft sputterings. Now shouts, sharp shrieks, harsh flutes
could wake you even from your final sheets,
propped pillow by hot window, parakeets.
In their high dance, from sky of helpless blue,
do green, dipped tails flash by you? Yes. They do.

Beneath Battersea Bridge

Who, from my fresh dead, said to me
that by the Severn he saw a tree,
a cormorant on each branch? I
sat through a play which made me cry,
as raw and piercing as lost time,
then walked below the plane trees' line
to the rough Thames. How the sky glowered
from satellite discs on Millbank's towers,
how traffic growled through Pimlico,
our ruined earth in final glow.

'Disused Power Station,' my map said.
There, as I turned my startled head,
a cormorant, feet skewed and wide,
swerved from rain's air, the plains of tide,
plunged down, to dark. Next two, then three
bobbed back, shook streamed black feathers free.
One small sail tacked past bridge's span
tracked surge and shimmer no hand can
enclose. Where should we meet? The dead
broad tree where Severn sweeps banks, he said.

All March

So in the frozen spring
the grey air sat above.
East wind would sometimes swing
to north. The quiet rich
flew off to Tenerife.

The fieldfares did not fly.
They crowded on the hills.
Birds fought for food. Harsh cries
drifted like feathers. Still
they tore dead grass to nest.

I found a sprig of twig,
broken, by bird or frost,
thumbed tawny with lichen,
saw that its scales had thrust
apart, so fetched it in.

It floated into sun
with yellow flakes of leaf,
small amber-whiskered flower,
wild plum's snow, dropped before
they flew from Tenerife.

MICHAEL CURTIS

Other

It was always there
this other that went with him
perhaps light, perhaps sinister.
They met from time to time
to conjure midnight or noon
the door to better dreams
a trap for his worst fears.
He suspected it was him
this other, that he must travel
through it to himself
had to go through
life's immense alternative
to the one place where
cold light clipped his shadow
and left him lean. Singular.
There he would stand alone
for the brahminy kite to sky
behind dappled palms
for the blue morpho butterfly
to waft huge and languorous
between waking pollens
while the drawn horizon
was crayonned red and yellow.
First feelings would regain
their glow, showing him
the verbs and nouns and articles
for it all, for it all
to make the right sort of sense.

KATE FOLEY

Fruit Harmony in the Dark

Bonnard, 1910

Most of us shed our skin
by careless increments,
not caring where the flakes drift,
what mites nibble the perfect
skeleton of cells.

Not Marthe. He tried,
baptized with light
the helpless flow of her substance,
moored her body
with a sacramental rope
to the hard white enamel of the bath.

Shadows bandage the wound of light,
and Marthe, whose nose is red,
whose skin is wrinkled, whose hair
is flattened by scented steam,
dies gently into her icon.

Elsewhere another frame,
a table set with red checked cloth
and round bread, a window
opening out – and once in the half light,
fruit, glowing hard and dark
as bitter chocolate.

Paris Church

Two very old women
bundled chin to belly in prayer,
a young woman texting in a pew

as the eye of god, faded and cracked
with age, stares down
from a window.

In this multi-lingual place
where prayer is a shaft of sun
on rubbed stone,

a wet foot-print where the mop
of the cleaner has drizzled
rainbow soap,

where coins clunk in a tin, a match hisses
and candles speak a little, uncertain
leap of intercession,

on the dry land at the other side
of grief, I am at last
able to mourn the loss of tears.

Only To Be There

Neat but for the white hair
that struggles out of her bun,
an old woman on the Paris metro
has a plastic bag at her feet.

Suddenly it heaves and bulges.
She leans her face toward the opening.
I see two fat, ordinary pigeons,
a small flutter at the edge

of their wings. One lifts
its ruffled neck, stretches
it's beak to her face. Beak
and lips meet.

Does she run a hospital
for pigeons with crippled feet?
Do they deliver messages?
How rare and strange

might it be to know
that you are utterly there
only for two pigeons in a bag
on the Paris metro?

CHRIS DODD

Change of Light

Frost hollows and fog-ponds,
bracken on the sun-slope copper-coined
and that scent of muck and alcohols,
the quiet urgency of blackbirds, wrens,
fresh humus being worked by quick orange mites,
springtails, protrurans,
eating, eating,
before the yellow of an approaching shower;
this slow hurry
of wild clematis on hawthorn,
of each blackberry ripening to its own flavour;
this fast, rich sleepwalk now,
the earth heavier, the air lighter.

The Northern Lights

Beyond the grain-dryer barn, out past Durno, green wavering searchlights are sweeping slowly – a thin curtain in the ionosphere. I call and you come out too and we stand there. Almost a frost. Somewhere, one of the pheasants shifts on its night perch. There's a rich smell of silage. Directly above us, if you stretch your neck back, the Milky Way, a great swath of outer spiral – all that time as light. Here the whole yard feels electrical, charged, a current running through us, through our sparse rare-earths. And a hint of that late summer smell from the field edges that were left uncut, our hands getting cold, tingling more when we touch, become some wider pole. Behind the propped-up gate there's a *fhooo* from one of the bullocks blowing.

The Measuring

This continuous ecstasy of photons
and each replying blade of lawn
darker-green stripes
where the mower wheels rolled
and over it all the roof's apical shadow
pyramided out across the drive's shingle
23 degrees C at 52 degrees North
Four varieties of tomato plants
are grow-bagged along the old stock wall
storing the day's heat
How little I want
How much I want

Among Beech Trees

That sound under your shoes
the smell of humus
soil crumb
sun on smooth trunks
on leaf drifts
curls of beech cob among
the cables of roots
how it gives under-foot
And in this light
something you glimpsed
when very young
but couldn't name
then or now

K. E. DUFFIN

House at Scituate

The dead would love it here.
Light surging in off the sea,
a hoard of weightless silver, a clear
view of clouds like fresh laundry
strung across panes of blue,
sand planed down to the ever-new
lace of frothing surf. Yes.
Where they belong, and could feel the caress

of floorboards beneath their feet, find
steps gently spilling to the waiting beach.
But it's all beyond their reach.
Their bodies gave out, were left behind.
None of it was planned.
New, vigorous bodies race the sand.

Rubythroat

I have some coldness, fear, like a marker.
You, sun spackler and sparkler,
tiny *orans* figure in iridescent
malachite, wearing your lifelong vestment,

materialize, suspended in air, whirring
before me, like those homunculi that pass
right through the windowglass
in Netherlandish paintings, bringing

the Holy Spirit into a mundane room.
Let us pray to the god of nectar.
When you turn to the many-belled altar
of purple flowerets that plume

the heart-leafed greenery, and show
your rippling, metallic back, each feather
a lens trebling the glint and glow,
you warm my doubt, my arctic weather,

with combinatorics, revealing dissolution
as only the *verso* of dazzling annunciation.

RHIAN EDWARDS

The Gulls are Mugging

The gulls are mugging the scholars again.
They're stalking lunches on parade, making nests
of hapless human scalps. It is then they unhinge
their jaws and snatch the booty whole, broad
daylight poaching from your unwelcoming hand.

Don't let the dove feathers fool you,
the slapstick march or the witless China
doll eyes. They could shawl their plumage
around you like a burlesque stole, smokescreen
you away into the perfect vanishing act.

They can dip bread in the ocean, baiting fish
into their tricking beaks. They have no qualms
pecking chunks from a whale hide when it surfaces
to breathe. They mate for life to rival the romance
of the swan, taking turns to brood until the chicks fledge.

Far from birdbrained, this is organised crime:
These rogue pickpocketers, mob raiders, white-suited
butchers. And they have all the elements covered:
these camp criers of the skies, fishwives of the seas,
unpacified foul mouths of this concrete square.

Murmuration

A scattering corralled, lassoed
into the universal doodle of birds,
a mutable speech bubble

of pondering 'm's. This is the bombast
of starlings as they corkscrew the sky.
Each twist and fold summarises them

to a simile, like iron filings,
being flocked and flung across the sky
by the metaphorical whims of a magnet.

Can you hear the pathetic fallacy?
The siren song of a metal's hum
crooning behind clouds, a bit like a God.

Return of the Native

The wooden bench is sinking, reclining
back to nature, reassuming root
in the cradling earth. Long grasses
have ambushed the concrete feet,
jaded mosses upholster the wolfing rot.

The latitude of the grain, the benchmark
of time when it thrived, is fading now.
Arrowed nettles loom through the parallel
cracks, their evangelical hands
cushioning the horizontal plain.

Even as a fraction of its elemental self,
it is defying the guise, the grand design
and callous return to earth. It shrinks
to its knees in the quickening soil,
swallowed by the shade of what it once was.

Soon the camouflage of this pew
will be absolute. And the skeletal fingers
of cow parsley that have locked their grip
to its backbone, will drag it back
to the grave where the ascendancy began.

ROSE FLINT

from *Lunar Station*

Ashes and Dust

(Anna, an engineer, speaks)

Mikos, on brief secondment from the Earth,
equates our quietness to absence of events.
Every night he wants a happening,
action, communication, loudness in his ears,
our voices wrangling and tense, he wouldn't care;
we are his symphony, his tangled line to home,
his defence against the loneliness of distance.

How our lives must shock him.
Is the moon so lit within our eyes that he sees us renegade –
half-things caught within the curious liminality of space?
We've slowed down, become monkish, thoughtful
as each day we find, measure, probe, take -
and every step we make across Selene's surface
becomes Event: a lessening of light.

The Beginning: chance or delicate design
birthing lunar light   fallen through furies only once
into such silence   utter   endless   windless   stillness
after violence
    last fire-fountain cooled, last rocks
resting into place,   particles settling
drifting   sheaf and mass   shaping
the architecture of a ragged, luminous pelt for Time

This regolith: fragile random heaps and towers of dust
arranged throughout these motionless billennia
    so each speck is balanced perfectly
        tiny facets offered to the Sun;
pagodas of infinity, holding out a million marvellous mirrors
                that disappear at a touch
as we stamp them shut, our clumsy boots as cudgels
killing beauty, staining moonlight dark

For Mikos, Moon is resource, boredom, opportunity.
He's made a game plan, set a backyard pitch
for balls and posts within the crater's field,
turned gravity around for profit. Back home he's saleable,
a leaping puffy giant with a boyish grin,
an extra-ordinary Joe who pays his tax and goes to church,
works hard to carry on his Mission far beyond celestial blue:

pushing out the boundaries of the human universe
to claim all that's useful on dead satellites and empty planets.
He'd say the Moon is big enough to take whatever
we might give it, as our vehicles terraform
the colles and fluctus, shape it to our purpose,
let our weight compress its useless surface.

On Earth they watch Moon mark the circling calendar of time
and do not see this locust-winter that we make here
– step by certain step – grow and spread like dusk
across her lustre. Always hungry, voracious now, we begin
to eat this lunar shining as easily as we melted snow
and turned midnight's reflections into ash.
From Selene, we've watched the icy landscapes
of the Earth grow fainter, her albedo dimming,
so Moon's reflective face falls deeper into shadow
and our long day grows colder, more sombre,
as earthshine that lit the old moon in the new moon's arms
fades down, so each crescent rinds only a greyer ghost of itself,
a blurred spindle turning broken light.

Mikos slams the ball he's loaded like a dice, lets it rip
around the crater. We watch it make a trick of gravity,
score a team point, so he lifts his fist in triumph, marks the gain.
Tomorrow, he'll explore untouched horizons
glassy glittered, black shadows deeper than ravines.
Earth will watch him, and the sun's unclosing eye.
We'll all trail in his wake, astronauts and politicians,
populations, planets, the universe of stars.
What we make and unmake here, is a first recording
of the alterations that we place in Time, both beyond
our home planet and within the heart of our existence;
as the changing luminous gaze that linked Earth to the Moon
become a memory, a troubled pull in the tide race
of our blood, a dream of loss we wake from in a sea of tears.

Welsh Church on the Hill

It sits in the valley like a boat
half-harboured in ewe pastures
where small oaks are wind-whipped
yellow sails, yearning for calm.

I'd step in to be rocked.
Inside, a good cradling, candled
by red-cheeked angels, smocked
in the comfort of Mary-blue.

But I'd light such a fuse
in this damp October weather
that old Doom would leap from the plaster
shaking his stick like a sacred rattle,
my sour fire and his glee puffing the air
out of the space under the rood.

Grim saints could do battle
for my thin, transient soul. Doom
doing his dance, while snarled dragons
licking my angry aroma, sleeked fast
as porpoises dipping through green weather;
last blood on the water

Oh those two angels in blue dresses
with familiar faces and fey hands.
Would they take me up and hold me
until the Spring came, bowing with light?
They know I am precious cargo and all at sea.

Snake in Quietness

A snakeman wound a boa round my waist
when I was sixteen, knowing nothing.
The thick silk heavyweight of its body
knotted me into its tight vital spiral;
no other animal could ever hold me so close.

Grown woman, a wild adder came to lie beside me
in the flaxen quietness of a summer height;
I stroked caressing fingers down his spine
felt his shiver response

and in that instant, became Eve, shocked awake
enough to receive serpent-wisdom
through the uttering leaves above us,
through flowers enquiry of light
through that moment compressed into my touch

when every separate world-view – *snake,*
woman, hill – coalesced, the universe rocking
in its black bed, world turning on its tree,
nothing separate, all connected
so my hand before my face is air and sun –
Nothing prepared me for how that knowing
pierced me, entered my blood. Changed me.

KAY COTTON

Walnut Tree

March: day and night a warbler,
a mocking 'Bastard Nightingale' imitating
notes of swallow, blackbird, others.

Noisy as a wren, he took cover as the tree
began to make buds, damp as butterfly wings,
torch in the mouth red. His song 'bursting out
occasionally very full and wild'.

July: small hard fruits push themselves
between a palimpsest of shady leaves
and through it, lichened trunk, patchy bark

mistaken for grazing cows on the rise
of the valley across the river. This fruiting tree
refutes my mother's saying nothing happens
in the country. Branches make waves.

October: deep-sea greens lap the tails of red squirrels
as they race and dive, harvesting. We unrolled a carpet
once, found a pillar of walnuts stored and forgotten.

When I'm gone,
there'll be another face at the window,
then another.
The tree will say nothing different.

Quotations: Bewick's *British Birds*, Vol. 1, p. 284

JOHN FREEMAN

My Father Swimming

Perhaps it doesn't need more understanding
than I've had of it all these years, seeing
in my mind's eye my father swimming
in a river where it passes between bluffs,
two occasions, fused: once when I, fifteen,
would have gone with him if I hadn't been sick
on the coach, and walked back to the hostel,
and once before even my brother was born.
I think of that as their real honeymoon.
When he went the second time he was alone.

He swam in solitude and became again
the man he'd been, young, hopeful, and in love,
and so serene and settled he looked out
as a baby looks outward from being fed,
engrossed in some object across the room
as in the focus for a meditation.
Happiness freed him to swim in the river
as if dissolving in the world around him,
slipping out of limitation and into
the water that received him, and the landscape,
the famous gorges they had come to visit.

She didn't swim in those days, she learned later.
I see her sitting on a rock, watching.
He would have felt her eyes on him, moving
with the water and against the water.
He must have felt them again, going back,
looking up at the sky above the cliffs –
I imagine them steep, a rich red colour,
like some I've passed through in the same country –
seeing the river stretch out deep and broad.
I think he must have worn the boundaries
of separateness as lightly as he wore
a single piece of cloth, or even less,
swimming naked, or almost, in his heaven.

Space Travellers

Ben and Eleanor live in Hinckley now.
Unexpectedly, like visitors from Mars,
they showed up at the door yesterday,
the third Saturday in January,
and sat with us in the warm living room
drinking tea and eating shortcake biscuits
from the tin they had given us for Christmas.
I kept looking at them, large as life, solid,
there in front of us, talking in voices
not heard for weeks, familiar as our own.
The cold gets in to all kinds of gloves, Ben said,
it will always find a way. When they'd arrived
we'd shaken hands and his had been like ice.
I photographed them as they rode off, waving,
on their brand new bike, all very smart,
distanced inside their astronaut helmets
in the clear but fading late afternoon.
The forecast was frost, and it didn't lie.
At ten they called to tell us they had landed.

ANNA LEWIS

At the George and Pilgrim

The small man in jeans and fleece
at the bar; his white pony-tail,
his pink skin. He talks to me
when I order, again when I go,
looks too long and too close –
there is something bloodless,
something of the dry leaves
and deep grass about him.

I'm here because it is old,
almost five hundred years old,
I've read. It rented out beds
to the pilgrims who came for the Tor,
for the Abbey and Bridget's poor chapel;
who walked after Patrick and David
and Gildas as though, if enough people

followed all in the same line,
if the right words were said
and right actions repeated,
a way might be worn
through this world to the next:
to the saints and the new shoots of Eden,
the lost and recovered dead.

And I walk behind them,
along the hard, bright afternoon:
up the Tor and back down,
in and out of the Abbey's wrecked arches,
around its fish-ponds, herb garden,

its orchard livid with plenty and rot,
where a near-horizontal light
weighs the branches, and each step
brings the soft jolt of apples
collapsing, sweetly, apart underfoot.

DOIRAN WILLIAMS

Triptych

1. Annunciation

Luca Signorelli

Always something divides them -
A gap in a stone wall,
A vase of flowers, a desk,
A pillar, or as here,
A parade of pillars.

He enters left, hovers,
Driven by words so urgent
They permit no time for
Feet to find purchase.

She sways backwards,
In a pas de Dieu
Where the dancers inhabit
Separate worlds, in suspense,
Until she speaks
The word of union.

2. Crucifixion

Cimabue

This ruined fresco puts Giotto
In his place, reverses Dante.
Havoc in the pigments has
Turned light into shade,
But we linger here longer
Than when we watched the saint
Preaching to the birds.
There is darkness over all
The land, the sun's light has failed,
But these wan figures
Will not let us go.
Mary and Longinus thrust arms
Like spears toward the Crucified;
Motionless, saints and sinners

Crowd the wings. Agitated angels
Hover, helpless.
Forehead to the wood,
Francis kneels.

3. Resurrection

Piero

Set aside the mastery of form;
It's the audacity that
Silences, the nerve to plug
The gospel gap, record the
Moment outside history,
The instant beyond legend.

No cave or boulder here,
No sign of angels,
His foot is planted hard,
Mid-stride, his hand gathers up
His robe, a hazard
For his trailing limb.

The wounds on hands and feet
Are dry.
The insult to his side
Still weeps.
His eyes look past us,
Ignore the prostrate guard.

A forward pupil queried
Why they slept.
"Not sleeping, but pretending,"
Said the master,
"Not tired, but terrified."
In the workshop, silence.

PHILIP GROSS

Frequencies

for Tig Sutton's High-Speed Art

Here's a sliver of air   as thin
as a microscope slide – scratched
there,   the stab, wince and back-
chat   of bat chitter – a glimpse
of the map   they can read   but
we . . .   (blind in that sense of theirs
in which they blur and veer, that we
can't name)   . . . we can't. To them
we are the dumb hulks of the night.

It doesn't forget, the cut wood,   not
the chainsaw or the sawmill, not the
carpentry,   nor the tiny indentations
where the man who wrote the book
leaned,   inking the marks by which
already   he has been forgotten –
leaving only this,   as a crop-shadow
centuries on remembers a lost city –
his true lifework in the mind of wood.

Tuning in to gnat frequencies, that
hour of evening, side-lit by low sun
when the hither-and-thithering   zip
and contra-zip of near-transparent
insects over water seems a kind of
stillness   poised
on the rip-curls of (breaking) sound
waves.   Silent.   Pipistrelles graze
leisurely as if down aisles at Tesco.

The slow spatterdash   speed paints
on your windscreen – no,   not grit
or the smatter of sleet   but road kill
at the finest level,   the oh-so-elegant
last words of things that lived   quick
and away   without weight   without
language and   in death   become this
dense script you squint into.   You'll
decipher it, if it's the last thing you do

Or see us, from the speed of a tree:
what can we be up to,   shuttling
between locations?   But the trees
have theories: are we particles or
waves?   (They note: we do break
now and then.)   Or dull collisions,
with that knucklebone clunk, click of
the Geiger counter – jiggling (how
bored is He) of God's quantum dice?

And now to walk into, and through, the
picture plane, into the long dimension
like a rank and splash-tagged subway,
or where   you ducked into the thicket
that only you knew about, and through
tacky spiderthread, creeper and words
like *impassable*, deeper than the wood
was long   into the silence, no time,
blank page waiting for a great surprise.

96

Tig Sutton   High Speed Art

'From Peterborough to the Emirates'   2012

'From Newark Northgate'   2012

'South of Peterborough'   2012

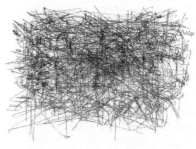
'Inter-city Blue'   2008

'Near Barnet'   2010

'From Lincoln' 2012

All these drawings were created in response to travelling on high speed train journeys between London and Lincoln. They were made by looking out the window at anything that attracted my attention and had to be drawn very quickly before the next thing grabbed my attention enforcing a kind of visual shorthand, whilst not looking down at the paper to check where or how the marks were appearing. This gives a compressed overview of a journey, taking sometimes up to an hour and a half, with the emphasis on the exhiliration of speed and complexity of modern life. Though done with a modest ballpoint pen, the marks, when enlarged many times take on a dynamic, gestural and very personal quality.

Leading into Strangeness:
Rowan Williams, Poet and Theologian

JEREMY HOOKER

Eamon Duffy, the Roman Catholic historian, paid a special tribute to Rowan Williams during his incumbency of the see of Canterbury, calling him 'its best theologian since St Anselm'.[1] Rowan Williams is not only a former archbishop, and a leading theologian; he is also a Swansea poet, like Dylan Thomas and Vernon Watkins. Influenced in earlier work by both, he has more in common with Watkins than Thomas. He describes Watkins as 'a "metaphysical" poet: that is, he aims to make visible something behind the surface of things'.[2] This may also be described as making strange, or revealing the strange within the familiar. As well as being a poet, Williams has written extensively about poetry and poets, including George Herbert and Henry Vaughan, David Jones, T. S. Eliot, and R. S. Thomas. He has translated Rainer Maria Rilke and several Russian poets. His translations of Welsh poets include Ann Griffiths and Waldo Williams. In general, we may assert that Williams writes a dense, allusive modern poetry that, while influenced by Eliot, Geoffrey Hill and R. S. Thomas, still possesses its own clear voice.

'Advent Calendar' gives a good idea of the sound of a Rowan Williams poem:

> He will come like last leaf's fall.
> One night when the November wind
> has flayed the trees to bone, and earth
> wakes choking on the mould,
> the soft shroud's folding.
>
> He will come like frost.
> One morning when the shrinking earth
> opens on mist, to find itself

<hr>

1 Eamon Duffy, 'Back to the cross', *Times Literary Supplement*, August 5, 2005, p. 25.
2 Rowan Williams, Foreword, *Vernon Watkins, New Selected Poems*, ed. Richard Ramsbotham (Manchester: Carcanet, 2006), p. ix.

arrested in the net
of alien, sword-set beauty.

He will come like dark.
One evening when the bursting red
December sun draws up the sheet
and penny-masks its eye to yield
the star-snowed fields of sky.

He will come, will come,
will come like crying in the night,
like blood, like breaking,
as the earth writhes to toss him free.
He will come like child.[3]

This may remind us of T. S. Eliot's 'Journey of the Magi': 'this birth was /
Hard and bitter agony for us, like Death, our death'.[4] In Williams's poem the
'hard and bitter agony' is in the sounds of the words as well as in the imagery
of death and torture: 'flayed the trees to the bone', 'choking', 'shroud', 'dark',
'breaking'. The seasonal images carry biblical allusions, and the poem is simultaneously harsh and hopeful. The insistent repetition of 'He will come' under-
lines the certainty that God will come. But the coming will be a violent rupture
in nature, 'like blood, like breaking, / as the earth writhes to toss him free'. It
will be a shattering of worldly assurances, and death to what is considered life.

The poet as preacher speaks in Williams's 'Advent' sermon, in which he
alludes at once to Rilke and Robert Southwell: 'Christmas is a beauty that is
the beginning of terror: the Burning Babe, who has come to cast fire upon the
earth. Before his presence, the idols fall and shatter'.[5] He describes Advent as 'a
word spoken, a word of unexpected interruption'.[6] The language of 'interruption', of rupture, breaking, shattering, splintering, estranging, is common
in Williams's poetry and sermons. The word that interrupts 'establishes for good
the difference between the God we expect and the God who comes, a word
that shows us once and for all what an idol looks like in face of the truth'.[7]

---

3 *The Poems of Rowan Williams* (Oxford: The Perpetua Press, 2002), p. 15. Further quotations
from poems in this book will be designated *PRW* and included in the text.

4 T. S. Eliot, *Collected Poems 1909 – 1962* (London: Faber, 1963), p. 110.

5 Rowan Williams, 'Advent', *Open to Judgement* (London: Darton, Longman and Todd, 1994),
p. 7.

6 Ibid., p. 10.

7 Ibid., p. 10.

Tension characterises Williams's poems. His sermon glosses 'the Advent tension' of the poem, as 'a way of learning again that God is God: that between even our deepest and holiest longing and the reality of God is a gap which only grace can cross; otherwise we are alone again, incommunicado, our signals and symbols bounced back to us off the glassy walls of the universe'.[8]

The image of a glass-walled universe as a prison represents all that Williams opposes. Windows frame man's perspective on the world; mirrors reflect him back to himself. Both have to be broken to admit grace. Everything in the world conspires to keep God out. It is in breaking, and in broken places that Williams finds the action of God. As he says, 'It is only when false images of God, the world and myself have been broken that I can be truly free'.[9] The title of Benjamin Myers' fine book, *Christ the Stranger*, encapsulates Williams's theology. His 'vision of Jesus Christ is as an intimate stranger, crucified and rising up into the broken world of human experience'.[10]

The poet's struggle is with what obstructs the vision, especially language, and the self. In 'Poetic and Religious Imagination', Williams says:

> The brutal and overwhelming monologue which Yahweh addresses to Job and his friends is essentially a long statement of the utter alienness and inaccessibility of the order of the world to the mind of man, the impossibility of an ordered linguistic picture of it. If there are things which God alone sees ('where were you when I laid the foundations of the earth?') how can speech about them ever be possible?[11]

The possibility of speech about God depends upon recognition of its impossibility, and the breaking of false images.

Williams's thinking is Augustinian; it is shot through with a radical sense of man's fallenness, which calls both language and the self into question. He is acutely aware of 'the pervasive risk of self-serving that belongs to human beings in virtue of their fallen state, the shadow that language itself carries in a world of power, greed, and self-protecting images'.[12] As in his poem 'Dream' (*PRW*, p. 47), Williams first recognises the risk in himself and his language.

---

8 Ibid., p. 11.

9 Rowan Williams, 'The Dark Night', *Open to Judgement*, p. 99.

10 Benjamin Myers, *Christ the Stranger: The Theology of Rowan Williams* (London: T & T Clark, 2012), p. x. A particular strength of this outstanding book is its treatment of Williams's poetry as integral to his theology.

11 Rowan Williams, 'Poetic and Religious Imagination', *Theology*, Vol. 80, No.675, p. 178.

12 Rowan Williams, *A Silent Action: Engagements with Thomas Merton* (London: SPCK, 2013), p. 67

'Dream' exposes both world and self to a bitter irony, which, applied to himself, has a touch of dark comedy. Alert to the world's suffering, the poet shows a tormented political awareness: 'News of another ceasefire broken: Sarajevo? / Somewhere like that. I stammer'. What follows exposes the futility of the language that disguises the stammering and hides the crying, which are true responses. 'We are due next, at a seminar / on violence, held in a courtroom or a theatre / something like that.' Lack of specificity – 'a courtroom or a theatre' – points to the uselessness and confusion of the talking-shop as a response to endemic worldly violence and betrayal. Williams portrays himself with rueful humour in the speakers: 'One bearded, / articulate and reasonable, talking of victims, / tragedy, the pathos of God trapped in a world of risks. He sounds like dense stringed music'. The speaker sounds, in fact, like Williams in his poetry and some of his theological writings. The self-portraiture continues: 'I fall into step / with him or someone from the benches opposite / (theatre? chapel? parliament?), bearded, / articulate and friendly. We have much in common'. In this comedy of beards, Williams in his several public roles – clerical, academic, dramatic – is refracted. In all, he is articulate and reasonable. The roles are all worthy, and all futile: masks that protect the crying, stammering man from the reality of death.

I have described the humour as rueful, but this is hardly appropriate to the encounter with wasps that begin to sting him towards the end of the poem, which concludes: 'I know I am going to die'. This sounds despairing. However, the poem describes a dream, which is a self-enclosed drama in which the self plays various parts. Only with knowledge of the reality of death is there possibility of rupture, when meaning breaks in from outside. So the implication of 'Dream' is not nihilistic: that death is the end. Realization of death is the waking knowledge with which true life begins. 'Dream' shows how Williams, as a Christian poet, reverses worldly expectations, exposing the limitations of sense and reason, and transcending them. His way is to strip away illusions, to dislocate, and estrange. He can shock and discomfort, with an almost medieval sense of horror, as in 'Cockcrow'.[13]

This poem in five parts is characterized from the outset by a more than usually violent imagery:

> As if light's arrival
> were a brick splintering windows;
> as if it were
> bones poking in the gullet,

---

13 Rowan Williams, *Headwaters* (Oxford: The Perpetua Press, 2008), pp. 45 – 47. Further quotation from this book will be designated *H* and included in the text.

> pushing it out of shape, so that
> the retching cry falls
> from the beak in a cascade
> of fractures, rubble, shredded flesh;
> as if day's return
> were a running knot against the throat.

Biographical criticism is risky at best, but at times compelling. In 'Cockcrow' the extreme everyday violence would be hard to account for fully without reference to the fact that Rowan Williams almost died of meningitis in infancy and grew up experiencing acute pain and the concomitant mental agony.[14] But while the biography may help to account for the violence of the reaction, it must not be used to explain away the emphasis upon suffering, which belongs to the Christian awareness of Gethsemane and Calvary.

Here, again, is imagery of splintering and broken glass, which relates to Williams's theology of the 'dark night' drawing upon John of the Cross and T. S. Eliot. "If you genuinely desire union with the unspeakable love of God,' Williams has said, 'then you must be prepared to have your 'religious' world shattered.'"[15] And, again, with reference to Calvary: 'It is the total shattering of any image and expectations of God when we see God helpless to save his Son'.[16] Cockcrow, moreover, is associated with betrayal, as Peter denied knowing Christ ('I do not know the man', Matthew 26: 74, all biblical references are to the King James Version unless otherwise indicated). The imagery of the poem is integral to the Christian story, to which Christ's agony on the cross, and the agony of martyrdom are central. But its visceral quality – 'bones poking in the gullet', 'waking is to swallow / yesterday's broken glass' – surely recalls the mental and physical suffering of the young Williams. This doesn't explain Williams's Christianity; it has helped him to become an authentic Christian poet.

In 'Cockcrow' Williams, the Swansea poet, has written a sort of anti-'Fern Hill'. 'Cockcrow' takes some of the same elements as the Dylan Thomas poem – time spent with relatives in the country, dawn light, waking, cock crow – and recasts them. Instead of an ecstatic recollection of original innocence, shadowed by a sense of mortality, Williams evokes the terror of man's fallen state. He ruptures the time-bound world, replacing Thomas's 'chains', which bind both poet and nature – 'I sang in my chains like the sea'[17] – with imagery drawn from

---

14 For this information I am indebted to Rupert Shortt, *Rowan's Rule*: The Biography of the Archbishop (London: Hodder & Stoughton, 2008), pp. 29 – 30.

15 Rowan Williams, 'The Dark Night', *Open to Judgement*, p. 97.

16 Ibid., p. 98.

17 Dylan Thomas, 'Fern Hill, *Collected Poems 1934 – 1952* (London: Dent, 1952), p. 161. The parallels between the two poems with their radical opposition between original innocence and original sin surely indicate that 'Cockcrow' is a conscious riposte to 'Fern Hill'.

Charles Wesley's hymn, quoted as epigraph. Wesley's 'mercy's beams' at 'the day's return' become at the end of 'Cockcrow' 'the rope let down from mercy's beams / to lift us raucously into the fresh splintered air'. In Williams's Christian universe grace is a light 'splintering windows'.

Few poets could be less Romantic than Rowan Williams, or further from celebrating the pleasure which there is in life itself. But if he is far from Wordsworth, he also distances himself from the early influence of his fellow Swansea poet, Dylan Thomas, in a verse free of Thomas's lilting melancholy and nostalgia. In a way quite different from Thomas's debt to Donne, the tradition Williams modernizes is metaphysical: that of the broken man who acknowledges his complete dependence upon divine grace. Nothing is easy in Williams. Life in his poetry is fraught with tensions.

The sense of dislocation, in which language comes under great strain, can be seen in a comparison of Williams's and Tony Conran's translations of Waldo Williams's 'Mewn Dau Gae', which is one of the great religious poems of the twentieth century. Set in two fields of Waldo's native Pembrokeshire, 'Mewn Dau Gae' involves a religious experience in which a mysterious figure binds together a group of working neighbours. Rooted in Waldo's Quaker faith, it is at once a poem of Welsh national unity and universal brotherhood, centred on the presence of Christ.

Tony Conran produces in his translation, 'In Two Fields', a great poem in English. His version is rhythmically fluent, sonorous and noble in expression, as we see in these lines from the third verse:

> And when the big clouds, the fugitive pilgrims,
> Were red with the sunset of stormy November,
> Down where the ash trees and maples divided the fields
> The song of the wind was deep like deep silence.[18]

Conran assimilates the Welsh poem to a high-sounding tradition of English Romantic verse. His version exercises a calming influence, conveying a sense of restoration and reconciliation, with an awe and wonder that are reassuring. Rowan Williams's version is quite different, as we see in his translation of the same lines:

> Clouds: big clouds, pilgrims, refugees,
> red with the evening sun of a November storm.
> Down where the fields divide, and ash and maple
> cluster, the wind's sound, the sound of the deep
> is an abyss of silence. (*H*, p. 91)

---

18 Tony Conran, *Welsh Verse* (Bridgend: Poetry Wales Press, 1986), p. 289.

Williams gives the poem a jagged rawness, and emphasises the poet's 'new voice'—'call it the poet's', 'rising and spilling from its hiding place'. Rather than calming 'the troubled self', this is more startling, more unsettling, rhythmically and with words that surprise (for example, 'this shameless glory'). It is more immediate, more quickening. The title he gives his translation, 'Between Two Fields', also marks its distance from Conran's version. 'In Two Fields' contains the experience, concentrating it in the place. 'Between Two Fields' makes the setting liminal, an edge, or border, or threshold. As in Williams's own poems, the strange is revealed in the familiar.

Mike Higton interprets Williams's idea of 'the poet' clearly and forcefully:

> The poet knows that our normal ways of speaking are both what enable our life in the world, and what limit it – and so the poet travels to the borderlands of our language in the hope of helping us to discover ways beyond those limits, or at least ways to discover aspects of reality which we are not yet able to speak, and which pose to us a task of exploration and discovery.[19]

Herein the task of the Christian poet is especially challenging, since he or she is not, ostensibly, travelling to the borderlands of language, but working within the field of a known story with its own long-established language. In a secular age of failing religious symbols, however, no poet has a greater need to make it new.

'Emmaus' (H, p. 21) is based on the story in Luke 24: 13-32. On the day when the women discover the empty tomb, two disciples are walking from Jerusalem to Emmaus, when a man they don't recognise joins them. He reveals himself to them at supper as Jesus:

> And it came to pass, as he sat at meat with them, he took bread, and blessed it, and brake, and gave to them. And their eyes were opened, and they knew him; and he vanished out of their sight (Luke 24: 30-31).

How does Williams make the story come alive for us? For the two disciples the walk is first an experience that disturbs their seeing and hearing: 'I screw my eyes to see/my friend's face, and its lines seem / different, and the voice shakes in the hot air'. The difference affects their walking. Their 'feet / tread a shape . . . out of step'. Their normal way of being in the world is disturbed: 'we cannot learn / the rhythm we are asked to walk, / And what we hear is not each other'. This is the effect the stranger has upon them.

---

19 Mike Higton, *Difficult Gospel*: The Theology of Rowan Williams (London: SCM Press, 2004), p. 78.

> Between us is filled up, the silence
> is filled up, lines of our hands
> and faces pushed into shape
> by the solid stranger, and the static
> breaks up our waves like dropped stones.

Where we expect 'faces pushed out of shape', we read the surprising 'faces pushed into shape'. This may be glossed by words from a Williams's book about icons: 'the shape of our own lives is finally going to be in God's hands, not ours: . . . we don't know yet . . . what we shall be'.[20] Christ the stranger enters life to change everything. He can be known only in the sacrament: 'as / the food is set and the first wine splashes, / a solid thumb and finger tear the thunderous / grey bread'. While 'thunderous' shocks with its violent strangeness, the imagery of filling points to completeness. Williams's theology emphasises inclusiveness, the hospitality of the Church to all.

'Emmaus' may remind us of a passage in *The Waste Land*:

> Who is the third who walks always beside you?
> When I count, there are only you and I together
> But when I look ahead up the white road
> There is always another one walking beside you . . .[21]

Eliot's note refers us to the account of an Antarctic expedition, which told 'that the party of explorers, at the extremity of their strength, had the constant delusion that there was *one more member* than could actually be counted'.[22] This experience is hauntingly mysterious, but it is a delusion. By contrast, Williams emphasises the solidity of the stranger. This is no ghost, as in *The Waste Land;* 'the solid stranger' makes the ordinary unreal, and is a source of explosive energy.

'Emmaus' is a retelling of the Bible story that renews its truth. Williams, like the seventeenth-century metaphysical poets, and like the Bible, including Jesus's parables, uses nature to intimate the supernatural, and the elements to symbolise the sacred. Thus, the final line of 'Emmaus', 'and our released voices shine with water', uses the water symbolism that Williams frequently calls on to intimate the baptismal and regenerative waters, the 'rivers of life'. In 'King Lear' (*H*, p. 60), for example, one of the 'ten prospects' comprising Williams's 'Shakespeare in Love', water symbolism helps to bring out the Christian meaning in Shakespeare.

---

20 Rowan Williams, *The Dwelling of the Light: Praying with Icons of Christ* (Norwich: The Canterbury Press, 2003), p. 17.

21 T. S. Eliot, 'The Waste Land', *Collected Poems 1909-1962*, p. 77.

22 Ibid., p. 85.

Here, the subject is cleverly withheld until the end of line 9, where it is revealed as 'rain'. The preceding lines, we now realize, are saying what rain does not do: 'keep you safe', soothe wounds, such as Gloucester's when his eyes have been plucked out. 'It does not surrender to the reasonable / case for not risking everything' expresses, in negative terms, the risk it does take, beyond reason. In consequence the apparent negativity of 'Never. It will not. Never' becomes profoundly paradoxical in a Christian interpretation of Lear's dying words, and therefore of the play.

The rain of the poem represents the storm that strips Lear of everything. He has lost Cordelia. 'Thou'll come no more. / Never, never, never, never!' The cry of despair is followed by words that are profoundly enigmatic: 'Do you see this? Look on her, look, look, her lips, / Look there, look there!' The Christian interpretation of this is that Lear now really sees his daughter for the first time. Formerly the self-blinded Lear had not seen or heard her. Now he sees all that she means, and hears the significance of her silence. Williams uses the rain symbolism to the same end, divesting Lear of everything but rain itself: the waters of life, holy water. The paradox is that of an apophatic theology which uses words and images to point to a truth beyond reason and beyond human language.

Williams's poetic art is highly visual. He is not concerned with surfaces, however, but uses pictures or paints scenes to show what lies below or beyond them – what erupts through the surface, or the depth the surface opens onto. His interest in icons is directly relevant to this. Williams's theology of the icon, like his Anglicanism generally, is strongly influenced by Eastern Orthodoxy. Understanding of his way of seeing depends upon grasping the difference between image and icon, which are essentially the same word, but with meanings, in normal usage, that are diametrically opposed. Images are about seeing, with the agent as see-er. They place the ego in relation to a world over which the self has mastery. Icons are about being seen; they open to the divine energy, and shatter the perceiving ego's mirror-image universe.

Rowan Williams has written several books about icons, and he returns to the subject in many of his writings. In his book on Dostoevsky, for example, he describes Holbein's picture of the dead Christ as 'a kind of anti-icon, a religious image which is a nonpresence or a presence of the negative', and contrasts it to the icon, which 'seeks to confront the viewer / worshipper with a direct gaze informed by the divine light'.[23] In the same book he speaks of the capacity of Holy Images 'to retain in themselves the real energy of another world, trans-

---

23 Rowan Williams, *Dostoevsky: Language, Faith and Fiction* (Waco, Texas: Baylor University Press, 2008), p. 53.

mitted into the world of isolated and death-bound agents'.[24] Elsewhere, he says, icons 'open the world to the "energy" of God',[25] an expression favoured by Eastern theologians. The 'energy of God' is integral to the theology of icons, and central to Rowan Williams's poetry. Where he writes about icons, therefore, he reveals the springs of his own poetic vision. Thus, in *Ponder these things: Praying with icons of the Virgin*, he meditates about being:

> aware of the utter strangeness of God that waits at the heart of what is familiar – as if the world were always at the edge of some total revolution, pregnant with a different kind of life, and we were always trying to catch the blinding momentary light of its changing. That is what any icon sets out to embody and transmit.[26]

Williams's poems, by analogy with icons, teach us 'to look through into the deep wells of life and truth'.[27]

His poem 'Resurrection: Borgo San Sepolcro' (*H*, p. 26), treats Piero della Francesca's R*esurrection* as if it were an icon in its effect upon the poet. He is at once faithful to the painting and uses words and images to renew its meaning. This he does principally by importing a verbal metaphor into the pictorial image: Spring, warmth easing

> the lids apart, the wax lips of a breaking bud
> defeated by the steady push, hour after hour,
> opening to show wet and dark, a tongue exploring,
> an eye shrinking against the dawn.

As in several poems, the process Williams depicts is that of a difficult birth, with the energy of new life having to overcome resistance. Images embody the effortful force of Christ rising, and render his resurrection as a flood: 'the green implacable / rising'. This is 'his spring.' The soldiers, though, sleep on, greeting the dawn 'in snoring dreams of a familiar / winter everyone prefers'. 'Everyone' includes the reader, whom the poem places between the risen Christ and the sleeping soldiers, 'paralysed as if in dreams'. The poem is at once tense with the effort of birth, and vibrant with the energy of spring. It draws on biblical

---

24 Ibid., p. 208.
25 Rowan Williams, *Ponder These Things: Praying with Icons of the Virgin* (Norwich: The Canterbury Press, 2002), p. xv.
26 Ibid., p. xvii
27 Rowan Williams, *The Dwelling of the Light*, p. 5.

images: 'Light / like a fishing line draws its catch straight up'. Like the Bible, it finds its metaphors for the energy of God in nature, in spring, water, and light. It renews the religious language, rendering the resurrection as a violent action of breaking, pushing, and opening. Christ's eyes are 'ravenous / imperative', seeking to flood the world with love and healing, as the water symbol implies. 'We', reader and soldiers, prefer our dreams to God's reality. The violence characteristic of this and other Williams's poems is reminiscent of what he calls 'that imagery of a kind of divine violence beloved of Augustine and John Donne and others'.[28]

Williams draws on his Celtic heritage in a group of poems called 'Celtia',[29] and in other poems. Like his devotion to the Eastern Church, his Welshness provides him with sources from which to energize his English-language poetry and renew traditional religious imagery and symbolism. 'Our Lady of Vladimir' (*PRW*, p. 14), in which the subject is the most sacred Russian icon, the *Theotokis* ('Birth-Giver of God'), is a striking example. Whereas the icon is a static image, the poem emphasises the energy it contains, immediately dramatizing the force of the child: 'Climbs the child, confident / up over breast, arm, shoulder'. The mother is 'alarmed by his bold thrust'. For her, he represents fearful energy. Looking at the icon, we may think we are seeing as she does, but 'her immeasurable eyes' tell us we cannot fathom them. She is part of the mystery, crying 'from her immeasurable eyes'. '[W]e turn away/into the window of immeasurable dark.' Our seeing is in a glass darkly; we cannot measure the depth of her eyes.

'Our Lady of Vladimir' is a poem about the incarnation which uses metaphor to enable us to see it anew. For this purpose, Williams calls on his Celtic inheritance for the image of the mistletoe, associated with the Druids: 'O how he clings, see how/he smothers every pore, like the soft / shining mistletoe to my black bark'. Pliny states that the Druids called mistletoe 'all-heal'. It is a symbol of immortality, strength and physical regeneration; and its meaning is inseparable from sacrifice. Mistletoe's mode of being is a startling metaphor for the incarnation, since its seed is brought mysteriously to the tree, but without the tree it cannot grow. With his striking use of the metaphor Williams restores both mystery and divine energy to the icon of Mother and Child. The poem shows that the icon is at once very human, and depicts a sacred action and a sacred relationship.

For Williams, poetry works at the frontier or border of the ordinary. Its 'hopefulness,' he writes, 'comes from its familiarity with those areas where the ordinary is no longer taken for granted, and the wholly alien becomes capable

---

28 Rowan Williams, *Ponder These Things*, p. 38.
29 *The Poems of Rowan Williams*, pp. 74-78.

of being in some way seen and recognized'.[30] Penrhys, a council estate in the Rhondda Valley, might be described as ordinary, though it is also the site of a medieval shrine of Our Lady.

> The ground falls sharply; into the broken glass,
> into the wasted mines, and turds are floating
> in the well. Refuse.
>
> May; but the wet, slapping wind is native here,
> not fond of holidays. A dour council cleaner,
> it lifts discarded
>
> Cartons and condoms and a few stray sheets
> of newspaper that the wind sticks
> across his face –
>
> The worn sub-Gothic infant, hanging awkwardly
> around, glued to a thin mother.[31]

This sets the scene. Situation and language are harsh. This is a common 'edge' of our urban society, a place of waste, pollution, and hanging around. The language is tense, and the religious meaning is in the tension. The newspaper and the 'sub-Gothic infant' form a central opposition – worldly refuse and opinion sticking across the image of Christ. One may think of Eliot's 'men and bits of paper' in the London Underground scene in 'Burnt Norton'.[32] In Eliot, this is an image of futile fragments, but in the newspaper hiding Christ's face we see Williams's radical communitarian politics: mere 'news' obscuring the good news meant for all. There follows an image of 'Angelus Novus':

> Backing into the granite future, wings spread,
> head shaking at the recorded day,
> no, he says, refuse,
>
> Not here.

The image refers to Paul Klee's painting which has become identified with Walter Benjamin's 'angel of history':

---

30 Rowan Williams, 'Swansea's Other Poet: Vernon Watkins and the Threshold between Worlds', *Welsh Writing in English*, vol. 8, 2003, p. 119.

31 'Penrhys', *The Poems of Rowan Williams*, pp. 51-52.

32 T. S. Eliot, *Four Quartets* (London: Faber, 1944), p. 17.

His face is turned toward the past. Where we perceive a chain of events, he sees one single catastrophe . . . The angel would like to stay, awaken the dead, and make whole what has been smashed. But a storm is blowing from Paradise . . . This storm irresistibly propels him into the future to which his back is turned, while the pile of debris before him grows skyward. This storm is what we call progress.[33]

Benjamin's 'angel' despairs of what Christianity promises: 'to awaken the dead and make whole what has been smashed'. 'Penrhys' doesn't offer an easy riposte. It poses the Christ image against the angel of history, rather than simply replacing the one with the other. It offers a held tension. The difference is that the angel is a spectator while Christ, 'hanging awkwardly / around', participates in the scene, together with 'teenage mothers by the bus stop'. The reality underlying the fantasies of the young mothers, behind the newsprint, is that of 'the bloody stubbornness / of getting someone born'. This painful bloody newness is as much at the heart of Christianity on Penrhys council estate now as at Walsingham in the Middle Ages. 'Refuse' is a key word. The ground here is refuse – waste. It is also what we might refuse, as we turn away in disgust and despair. But here the infant participates; as in the 'holiest place, the refuse tip, the rag and bone heap of Calvary, (whence) flow the streams that water the whole dry earth'.[34]

In his poetry Rowan Williams depicts situations or suffering in which the world is 'on the edge of some total revolution, pregnant with a different kind of life'. He writes in the tradition of what he calls 'Anglican identities', shared by figures such as Richard Hooker and George Herbert.

> They know that as Christians they live among immensities of meaning, live in the wake of a divine action which defies summary explanation. They take it for granted that the believer is always learning, moving in and out of speech and silence in a continuous wonder and a continuous turning inside-out of mind and feeling.[35]

Williams's particular affinities are with the metaphysical poets in this tradition, with George Herbert's irony and Henry Vaughan's mystery. He defines irony as 'the careful subversion of language itself by trailing through your discourse

33 Walter Benjamin, 'Theses on the Philosophy of History', *Illuminations,* ed. Hannah Arendt (London: Jonathan Cape, 1970), pp. 259-260. I am grateful to my friend, Rev. Canon Stephen Batty, for our discussions of 'Angelus Novus' and of Rowan Williams's writings generally.

34 Rowan Williams, 'Holy Ground', *Open to* Judgement, p. 137.

35 Rowan Williams, *Anglican Identities* (London: Darton, Longman and Todd, 2004), p. 7.

the signs of questioning and incompletion'. By mystery, he means 'the creation of language that always suggests a pregnant depth, occasionally discernible but always under the surface of what is said'.[36] These are not hard and fast opposites, describing two different kinds of poetry. 'I suspect,' Rowan Williams says, 'that all good poetry, and especially all good religious poetry, moves between irony and mystery'.[37]

Williams renews the tradition of Christian poets, such as Herbert and Vaughan, who not only stress the inadequacy of all human language to carry the meaning of the Cross, but sometimes mock or deconstruct that language in order to reveal the truth it conceals. Williams, in turn, occasionally exposes the rare linguistic hubris of his great metaphysical predecessors, as when, in 'Jerusalem Limestone', he takes the triumphant closing words of Herbert's 'Prayer' 2 and adds a 'not': 'Something not understood' (PRW, p. 59).

Williams's apophatic theology reflects scepticism not only of religious language but of the power of the human mind. As a thinker he has responded sensitively to the exposure of power structures, not least in religious language and institutions, by feminists and postmodernists. 'Easter Eve: Sepulchre' begins: 'Constantine knew, of course, just what he wanted'. The emperor is identified with knowing, and with wanting and making, with 'space for cool power' and 'a new, enlightened holy hill'. For the present–day pilgrims, of whom the poet is one, it is different:

> Saturday afternoon, the bodies squashed, wet, boxed,
> breathing into the shadows full of smells and tinsel;
> flame leaks and spits out of the singularity,
> sparks a cracked bell. Iron, rope, smoke
>
> Pant in the tight dark, a light-footed,
> high-strung passing. Afterwards we breathe,
> dry off the sweat and crying, ask what history
> is after, bullying us into waking, into this oppositeness. (PRW, p. 61)

These lines are characteristic of Rowan Williams: the particularity of the occasion; the sheer uncomfortable compacted humanness of the faithful; the use of a special term, 'singularity', to refer to Christ's sacrificial death; the double meaning, reminiscent of Geoffrey Hill, in 'what history is after'. Material words, 'sweat and crying', refer to the Passion, which the faithful commemorate, and

---

36 Rowan Williams, 'The Mystical Tradition in Anglicanism: Thoughts on Herbert and Vaughan', *Temenos Academy Review* 2008, p. 143.

37 Ibid., p. 153.

are thus woken into 'oppositeness'—witness to a reality that contradicts the reasons and power of empire.

The use of 'singularity' recalls R. S Thomas's use of scientific terms in later poems. In the Preface to the first edition of *The Wound of Knowledge*, whose title is drawn from Thomas's poem 'Roger Bacon', Williams writes that Thomas 'has long since said most of what I want to say'.[38] This is a modest disclaimer of originality, but it is open to question in several respects. Principally, Williams does not share the exclusive nationalism of Thomas's romantic concept of Welsh-speaking Wales. Williams's Church is notably a 'broad' one, in the sense that it seeks to make room for the world.

Society and community matter to Rowan Williams. In *On Christian Theology*, he speaks of 'our fundamental need, which is for identity in relation, conversation, mutual recognition'.[39] One may think in this context of his Welshness and his affinity with Raymond Williams, but he belongs equally to the tradition of John Ruskin and William Morris, and to that of Russian religious thinkers, such as Sergius Bulgakov. There is an angry and oppositional man behind the cleric's gentle exterior, a man who in *Lost Icons* articulates 'anger . . . at a recent history of public corruption and barbarity compounded by apathy and narcissism in our imaginative world'.[40] He is a fierce critic of our 'cultural setting where depthlessness looks like becoming normal'.[41]

Williams returns again and again in his writings to the need of the Church to represent the comprehensiveness of the Redemption. The theme stretched David Jones's generous imagination, and he symbolized it by the ship in *The Anathemata*. In 'Thomas Merton 1966' (*PRW*, p. 49) Williams also renews this traditional symbol. Merton, at a crisis in his life, is described as 'once-fluent fellow', who has 'made a landfall, emptied on to the shore / gasping and heaving against a new hard element, / against the solid sand'. The 'hard element' recalls the Jerusalem landscape, literally and metaphorically. Reflecting both on his own youthful perception of Merton and Merton's actual contemporary experience, the poet says, 'Not to make sense is / what most matters'. The poem concludes with the same recognition:

> Not to make sense, inside the keel of sweating ribs,
> not to make sense but room.

---

38 Rowan Williams, *The Wound of Knowledge* (London: Darton, Longman and Todd, 1979), p. x.

39 Rowan Williams, *On Christian Theology* (Oxford: Blackwell, 2000), p. 71.

40 Rowan Williams, *Lost Icons*: Reflections on Cultural Bereavement (Edinburgh: T & T Clark, 2000), p. 9.

41 Rowan Williams, *Dostoevsky*, p. 229.

Compassion, the Church as a hospitable body, with all that that implies in material and social terms, and in terms of human particularity and painful love, requires something different from 'sense' with its instruments of verbal and intellectual fluency. It requires of the poet being-in-the-world, as the Cross is, in the hardest, most violent and deprived places, and in the 'darkness' of the human heart. Thomas Merton's Church, that of the 'sweating mariners', is the one of which Rowan Williams is a member, 'in the heart of a needy, contaminated, messy world'.[42]

Two words that might be used to sum up Williams's poetry are incompleteness and energy. Incompleteness suggests brokenness. 'In suffering,' Williams wrote in *The Wound of Knowledge*, 'the believer's self-protection and isolation are broken: the heart is broken so as to make space for others, for compassion'.[43] Luther's restatement of the tradition of negative theology supports this idea: 'God himself is the great "negative theologian", who shatters all our images by addressing us in the cross of Jesus.'[44]

Incompletion both marks the limits of reason and language, and points to a pattern, a structure, a story that completes our partial being. This is what Williams means by what he calls Dostoevsky's 'theology of writing', which is applicable to poetry: 'Every morally and religiously serious fiction has to project something beyond that ending or otherwise signal a level of incompletion, . . . indicating an as yet untold story'.[45] There is always a depth below what we see, and a story beyond our telling.

Rowan Williams's Anglicanism has been hugely energized by his early study of Eastern Orthodoxy and his devotion to icons. While R. S. Thomas calls on metaphors from Modern physics to furnish his 'Laboratories of the Spirit', Williams relates scientific discoveries to 'the energy of God':

> The scientist, of course, will tell us that at the heart of every apparently solid thing is the dance of the subatomic particles. The theologian ought to be delighted that this sort of talk puts movement and energy at the centre, but will want to add that at the heart of the subatomic particles is an action and motion still more basic, beyond measure and observation – the outpouring of life from God.[46]

---

42 Rowan Williams, *Being Christian* (London: SPCK, 2014), p. 6.
43 Rowan Williams, *The Wound of Knowledge*, p. 12.
44 Ibid., p. 149.
45 Rowan Williams, *Dostoevsky*, p. 46.
46 Rowan Williams, *Tokens of Trust* (London: Canterbury Press, 2007), p. 36.

David Jones's priests, ('these rear-guard details') at the beginning of *The Anathemata,* continue celebrating Mass heedless 'that dead symbols litter to the base of the cult-stone'.[47] Countless Christians around the world continue to find the traditional language of their religion adequate to their needs. It is different for poets and artists, for whom faith itself may depend upon their capacity to make it new. In this context, we may reflect that there can be no great modern Christian poetry that is not a channel for this energy—'the outpouring of life from God'. Subjective emotion alone doesn't do it. Nor does conventional use of Christian language and imagery. Energy, however, doesn't come without emotion, but the emotion must be a 'refining fire', a formal and linguistic process of destruction and making new. Little modern poetry in English meets this requirement, and that which does is seldom orthodox.

More sacred energy is being perceived in nature, especially by women poets. 'Spiritual' is a vexed term for modern theologians, something they associate with a vapid and self-indulgent New Ageism. But in some poetry the mother-power of creation is an eruptive force, and a healing influence. There is an idea of the female in Christianity – in sentimental images of the Virgin, for example – that denies life-energy and needs taking back to the generative principle, as David Jones does in *The Anathemata.* For all his admiration of Jones, Williams is in some respects a distinctly masculine poet, like R. S. Thomas. Unlike Thomas, however, he embraces the messily human. Moreover, imagery of pregnancy and birthing is integral to his incarnational poetry.

For Williams, as an exceptionally gifted thinker with a powerful intellect, it may be a special necessity to humble the power of reason, first of all in himself. It may be, also, that coming close to death and experiencing agony in childhood proved on his pulses the utter powerlessness of the human mind unaided by grace. Apophatic or negative theology, which he defines as 'the principle that whatever is specifically said of God has also to be un-said as soon as it seems to offer the seductive prospect of a definition of the divine essence', is rooted in his being.[48]

In Williams, as in his great metaphysical predecessors, we see how in his and the world's brokenness he apprehends the energy of God. We see how his Christian poetry, like theirs, makes original use of nature to symbolize the supernatural. In this it is biblical, for the Bible leads into strangeness, whether with burning bush or dove descending, that represents the Holy Spirit. In Williams's

47 David Jones, *The Anathemata* (London: Faber: 1952), p. 50. Rowan Williams's profound affinity with the thought of David Jones, and admiration for his poetry and painting, find expression in several of his writings, most notably in the extensive treatment of Jones in *Grace and Necessity*: Reflections on Art and Love (London: Continuum, 2005).
48 Rowan Williams, *Dostoevsky*, p. 59.

poetic development we see the influence of fellow Swansea poets, Dylan Thomas and Vernon Watkins. In his work too, as in theirs and that of Welsh-language poets, we see the estranging spirit of Celtic symbolism that animates his English poetry. He is a metaphysical poet who 'aims to make visible something behind the surface of things'. Crucial in this respect is his theology of the icon, which brings to his poetry awareness 'of the utter strangeness of God that waits at the edge of some total revolution, pregnant with a different kind of life'.

Emiko Aida, *Pram*

DAVID HART

The Border Sketchy

Bronwen says she sees no trace of work done.
Morgan says it's all trodden in, *You'll see.*
When *you* are asleep I shall come out and drill holes.
In your dreams, you Bronwit flotilla of wrinkles.
Mustn't turn in ourselves, Morgue, we must
stay on the attack, break some windows.

God knows what it is in them and in me,
how it goes with us gods here on the turn always,
how obsolete the prayers and how necessary.

They set about smashing my autobiography,
lay chicken feed across all my carpets,
erect signs saying I hadn't done my homework.

It would be something if they'd plot quietly,
they hop around my breakfast table
conducting the music of the spheres upside down.

They welcome me home from the office by having
painted over my windows with chocolate custard.
I shout, I cry, I plead, they laugh as if they are angels
after strenuous blessing, on my head fluttery,
I try to explain good manners and earthy kindness,
this makes then kick each other, leaving a trail of blood.

I am vulnerable to their masks made from skin
torn off rabbits. Back then I could set them
against each other outside with mud and nettles.
It helps me to imagine I could do that, one day
the thought of it made me laugh. Must be good
if I could properly master it. They seem to have no
formality. Could I teach them lyric poetry? Yes,
if I could anaesthetize them for, say, five years.

117

Let's conclude this with a prayer, shall we, kneeling?
Come, friends, let us collude as light from fire,
see how affection binds us, reminds us: we *are us*.

Here they come brandishing neon tubes
full of sulphur light, they ask me to sign their
Doctrine of Smudged Blessings Delirious.
I say I will not, I say there is a limit, I say please
         don't do it.

RICHARD HAWTREE

Stray Versicles

I *after* Colmán of Cloyne

I do not wake to a weak stanza
after lush and dream rich sleep:

my verse is rest from a Lenten fast,
grace distilled from Christ's own cask.

II *after* the Anglo-Saxon '*Guthlac* poet'

That is the turning of love's gates
when in our hearts she elevates

those gifts of spirit.
Even her master bids us drink –

to think
and let love sink

right through –
making our hinges new.

III *On an Irish Psalter raised from Faddan More bog*

So up with you then illuminated bird
singing a new psalm from soft Faddan More,

your plumage stiffened with ink,
your hooked beak riddled with peat.

Beatus-bearing
bog swathe

struggling from the hand-made
word slick.

W. D. JACKSON
from *Shakespearean Sonnets*

viii

Love's Labour's Lost – Berowne

When shall you see me write a thing in rhyme?
Or groan for Joan?

IV.iii.177–8

We gave our word – a college of young *fools*
To swear that we'd just study for three years!
Obey a senseless list of monkish rules,
Make war against our own and the world's desires.

We play with words as if they were mere foam
Blown here and there by stormy nights or days –
In court, town, tavern, or in bed at home,
Desiring this man's hurt, that woman's praise.

Honey-tongued when it suits us, imprecise
And usually in disguise, let us here vow
To mean what our words say – straight no, plain yes –
And keep the things we promise . . . Except that, now,

Why should these French girls trust us? Or why we
Our shallow oaths' impure integrity?

x
A Midsummer Night's Dream – Hippolyta

Merry and tragical? Tedious and brief? . . .
How shall we find the concord of this discord?
V.i.58,60

– Or *make* the concord which we cannot find?
The story shall be changed – and changed again . . .
Till fantasy and reason, heart and mind,
Re-dream *themselves* . . . Poor women, poor moon-mad men,

Can see no further. But of all creation
We see the best. Theseus, as duke, thinks words
Can comprehend the truth! imagination,
Brief as forked lightning, hot as squabbling birds,

Disperse and leave cool, clear reality
To dawn! And yet what joy apt words can bring:
Though "laurel" is no laurel – "Daphne" no tree –
When beauty blinds us, words flash – fly – bloom – sing . . .

And all our minds', could they be heard together,
Might *be* the story of the night told over.

xvi
Much Ado About Nothing – Benedick

Come, lady, die to live; this wedding day
Perhaps is but prolong'd . . .
IV.i.253-4

Because our custom has not been to speak
The simple truth, how can we easily now?
Claudio is Hero's husband. Fashionable, weak,
What's 'love' to him but a word? What's in a vow?

Pedro's a prince, but neither strong nor wise –
A self-regarding wit, a shallow youth.
I play the merry fool in their blind eyes:
Show me the man who'll tell a prince the truth!

We hide and seek to hear what others say
About us. See ourselves in how they see us.
A change of heart – or mind – changes the way
We see things, say things. The Friar plotted to free us

From biting error. Can souls so giddy survive?
How much of all our *nothing* is really alive?

SEAN H. MCDOWELL

Wind at Dún Aonghasa

for Gib Rossing

Here in the innermost wall
it spades all the open places
and spreads across face and hands
like sunburn. Constant as water's
embrace, it softens a tour guide's
barked guttural German into
something like normal conversation.
It muffles the buzzing of horse flies
and the cries of gulls floating
like open books someone
fell asleep while reading.
It deadens the whoosh and crash
of surf below.

            And yet the longer
you listen, the more it resembles
circulation, the kind you hear when
you cover an ear with a water glass
or the flayed mouth of a conch shell.
Something larger than any of us breathes:
Here, where only shy things grow,
the wind is the voice the world
uses when neither you nor I
nor anyone else can interject.
It belongs in the gaps between
unmortared stones.

[handwritten annotations:]
innermost and largest, 3 tiers of stones
cliff
Altar?
can they fly in a Atlantic wind?
= the wind!
↓ v-sparse habitat,
↓ most famous of several prehistoric forts on Aran Islands, Co. Galway Is or Inishmore, at edge of 100m high cliff.

123

MAUREEN JIVANI

Dear God

For God's sake God almighty God willing
God forbid God given God knows God
help us at tables in cafes lifting tearful cappuccinos
for two years now
in God's name do not in vain dear God forgive us we don't
know we know dear God we are made frothy beard God protect us from
fruitcakes so Father where is my daughter mother father when we go where we
go no love dear abstract God dear God show us an eye a nose an ear god bless
a hand and singing amen amen amen

August

His words are a lullaby
    in my dreams:

they do not labour
under the lung's negative pressure.

*   *   *

I have been here all summer.
    The half-light filters through

shuttered blinds like the threat
    of snow.

*   *   *

He's tells me, 'There will be time.
There will be time'.

For what, dad?

'To set a watch.'

'To put the kettle on.'

*   *   *

The catheter bag fills – amber. Red.
'There's no poetry in that.' he says.

*   *   *

Once more I unstick his lips,
  ice his mouth,

sing to him – *Baby face.*
    Ah baby face . . .

OLIVER COMINS

Red Horse

At first it seemed
to be just
a chestnut horse,
gender unknown,
glowing in this
slippery winter
morning light.
A cluttered view,
being too close
to see any pattern
except long shadows
of trees, hedgerows,
a horse, shrinking
as a covert sun
continued to rise.

My train moving
nearer, the horse
became more red
than brown, more
mine than anyone
else's: I saw her
strong scarlet flank,
a tremor of muscle,
so close – a moment
and I was looking
into those russet eyes
beneath her purple
mane . . . my red
Red Horse, grazing,
limpid, in her field.

BRENDA LEALMAN

Exodus

St Kilda, 29 August 1930

Leaving you is to see
jags and gobs
turn to soft kelt,
to recall what is tender in you
the furl of intimacy
inside immensity:

clumps of wild iris
fleeces of mouflon sheep
umber ginger cream

the way grass is sappy round the cleits

how Dun, Red Fell, East Fell
enfold the village; the enclosing
lunate hills: rounded
East Fell and Beacon,
Big Top Bright Top
Pillar Top Cleft Top.

When HMS *Harebell* carried away
the St Kildans for ever they broke
and wept as the antlers of Dun smudged.

Did they think of your softnesses?
Of tender fulmar flesh as they ate
the beef offered on board?
Of slippers made from gannet throats
thickly lined with feathers?

Or, did they think of your harshness?
The stink of fulmar oil, the hits of
vile fulmar vomit?

Of women in the nettled
graveyard howling for their
babies dead at eight days old

for husbands who spun out on ropes
and fell whilst fowling from cliffs
at The Gap
   Shingle of the Skerry
Stac a'Langa
   Cowamberling?

Did they remember the wild
cries of Ivor's mother?
My son, my son,
You will not return to your mother
For mending of your shirt.

Italics: from a collection of St Kilda laments for men lost on the cliffs made by
The Revd Mackenzie and published in 1906.
Gob: Gaelic for beak, point eg pointed rock
Cleits: low stone structures with turf roofs used for storage and drying
English translations of Old Norse and Gaelic names have been used:

Old Norse
Red Fell   *Ruaival (val= Viking fjall hill)*
East Fell   *Oiseval*

Gaelic
Beacon   *Conachair*
Big Top   *Mullach Mor*
Bright Top   *Mullach Geal*
Pillar Top   *Mullach Bi*
Cleft Top   *Mullach Sgar*

Looming

What shook us
an hour after dawn
wasn't the night cold
still hovering over sea

but a seascape floating
across the sky
                moving
through cloudshadow
and slivers of silver

sea swinging upwards
lifting a boat so fleecy
that it scuffed against clouds

here there getting no where.

Had we feathered wings
to rise   row through sky?

Or some strange others?

We felt only our flimsiness
beneath oilskin trappings,
how skimpy the skiffs of self

tissue selvings
                wind glyphs
on gusts of cloud-ocean

address unknown

A Looming: name given by sailors to a superior (overhead) mirage at sea.

PATRICIA MCCARTHY

Bell Ringers

April 1914, St. Dunstan's church, Mayfield

Arthur Groombridge, John Thurlow, Basil Paine –
each of your bells polished by your pride
in the ringing chamber where you swung

from ropes as if from trees in Park Wood.
Every pull sent storms away from the ridge
to rumble around the valley, *striking*

your expertise. Heard there still, you splice
bell ropes, mutter numbers and names
Minimus, Minor, Major, Royal, Maximus…

Singles, Doubles, Triples, Caters, Cinques…
miniature thunder gods reciting what teachers
never taught, patterns and rows in beats

steady as the clop of horses along the High Street,
steady as your fit young hearts, the sap
in your veins that month from bluebell woods,

primroses and drifting blossom on your breath.
You should have stayed where wild orchids grew
at your feet, doing cartwheel call-changes,

calling up, calling down, swapping bells
in a Mayfield of mayweed, maypoles, maids. But –
escaped from St. Dunstan's tongs, a devilish clash

of shellfire in your ears silenced all bells.
How much better for you to have been killed
holding onto wet ropes in a local thunderstorm

while ringing that half peal of Grandsire Triples
to celebrate the new village school. Each clapper,
muffled fully now, evokes you with its elegies.

EDWARD STOREY

Seeing Music

How often you've been here but not here
When music becomes visible
And there's a presence in the empty space
Between the sound of one note and the next.

Is this what Rilke meant –
It's *a breathing of statues, perhaps. . .*
Or *stillness in pictures.?* Someone always
Comes to life when song becomes more than song.

But how difficult it is for one
To applaud for two. We'd prefer the silence
To remain intimate, for the last note
To delay meeting the note unsung,

For the statue to keep breathing.

Bringing Home a Nightingale's Egg-shell

(for Ann)

You cradled in the nest of your hands
Nearly the whole of a small shell
That had released its song to the sky.

Thin as an onion skin, it held
The soft white membrane of birth
Still mother-bird-warm and frail,

Too delicate for us to comprehend
How a song-bird grew from a brown pearl
To free itself on Hergest Hill.

And what of the song? Was it as fragile
As the shell your hands brought home?
The sky is such a hollow place to fill

Some songs are destined to die young.
Wings fail to reach where they would wish to fly
And all horizons tease the keenest eye.

Yet, while this shell, now like a tiny skull,
Sits on my shelf, its joy can never be
Silenced by predator or grief.

SEÁN STREET

Mass in E-flat Major*

i. Kyrie

Steps leading down into a black water.
The needle starts its probe, spiking tissue,
and the invasion asks its own questions.
I can no longer guess where matter ends
and spirit begins, the invisible
obscured by the physical, the thinking
concealed by the pain, which is its mercy.

ii. Gloria

Nant Gwrtheyrn

Water's edge then dark beyond us.
The words say one thing but the way
we say them is what reveals things.
The companionship of daylight,
that is enough to pray for now,
and it is somewhere far out there,
celebration of consciousness,
stones weathering storm then storm
before our bones reach their morning.

So you can see, when that light stings
the cold, it is the deep distance
that awes, defeats through unfathomed
space. You cannot help but wonder
now, faced with the pockets of blood

---

* 'Schubert's final mass was composed during the summer of 1828, only months before his death. In it, liturgical tradition is coloured by an individual and unsettling chromaticism, evoking the personal pain he was suffering, not only physically but also through the anguish of questioning his faith' (Programme note).

we are, nothing better to show
the truth of the ordinary,
the honesty of a morning
than empty skies.
What is there? Swim
until currents win. Little left
to be achieved, everything
to be attempted. Everything.

iii. Credo

One by one metal shutters,
gridlocks in evening rain
stop the city in the act
of heading out from the week
to material churches.

Pilgrims, it is the journey
and you are what you believe,
and what we believe comes to us
from an inventory we
make, patterns and acts of faith,
like trusting light to wake us.

Between prayer and promise
there is an uncertain light.

iv. Sanctus

The angels are accountable to sacred rules,
but I live as best I can in silence as thick
as fog, and still not understanding the purpose.
Pleni sunt coeli et terra gloria tua.
A memory then, to consecrate the places
that knew us, uncovering the layers under
new tides before the mind's pictures start to dissolve.

v. Benedictus

Coastal Erosion, Formby Point

The next high water claims back
what we called our own. Nothing
belongs and we own nothing,
what eats into us now, made
us, and so we have no cause
for complaint. That said, what eats
us is our sad envy of
unlived days, but I have seen
my children grow, so I have
no cause, no cause for complaint.

Sands give way under our feet,
a far rig's fire bleeds into
dark, the wind farm's choir tenses
for vespers and wings beat down
over me, heading inland.
Benedictus qui venit,
the airborne ice sends spirits
homeward. I flicker and fade.

vi. Agnus Dei

The air is full of textings
and a shrill plastic panic,
full of prayers and promise.
Have mercy on us. We seek
a permanent present, so
there's comfort in removing
history to make ourselves
eternally immediate.
This is close to accomplishment,
the sacred almost erased
by routine.

In my moment
I would wish to be somehow
a continuing partner
to the world and its selfness
with me, but nothing belongs.

I try to guess where matter
ends, where the spirit begins,
acts of faith, like trusting
the unheard and unclimbed,
the idea of Place,
love when it's shared, unseen,
existing notwithstanding.

HELEN MOORE

Honeydew at Solstice

For L

Sumptuous yellow melon, your globe inscribed with solar braille
recording radiant heat and light – how each solicited
this plumpness – a signature in pictogram by our incubating star
a hidden imprint where the ground supported you.

Melon de España, grown old school – no chemicals
to sour your flesh or foul your roots. With gratitude
we've sliced you through and take our spoons to scoop
the seeds from each succulent well.

Soon our teeth gnaw at the rind, juice tracing rivulets
on skin that still wears a smooth indivisibility from our river-swim,
and I'm recounting how I once ate pizza like an urban Fox,
on all fours tearing at the box on the floor,

discovering freedoms that cutlery denies us –
open mouth chewing, how air drawn in over the palate
releases a full spectrum of flavours, and we're laughing,
expanding with the Elderflower hock –

Wild Cr🅐fty Brew, made with spring water,
no additives or sulphites. Amidst the oppressions of this
so-called 'civilisation', our friendship is soul-food, and your poems
read by candlelight and a halo of Roses

are utterances that rain in like drops of honey –
these distilled articulations from a consciousness I love.
Later, as I sit beneath the Elder tree
which the neighbour hacked down last year,

its shady crisscross of branches once again bearing clots
of grey, sap-hungry Aphids, I can feel stickiness spitting on my limbs
as Ants 'milk' them with their antennae –
this corresponding hunger for honeydew at Solstice.

137

John Chatwin's Translations of Henry Vaughan

PHILIP WEST

This article focuses on two previously unrecognised translations of Henry Vaughan's Latin poems made between 1680 and 1685 by the Cambridge undergraduate John Chatwin. The translations of 'Ad Fluvium Iscam' and 'Ad Echum' survive in the author's manuscript verse miscellany, now Bodleian MS Rawlinson poet. 94, the relevant pages of which are given in semi-diplomatic transcription immediately after this introduction. Chatwin was only in his late teens when he produced the translations, but his English shows sensitivity both to the Latin originals from *Olor Iscanus* and to the language and style of Vaughan's other pastoral and Ovidian poetry. His versions of Vaughan are of particular interest since there is such limited evidence for the Silurist's seventeenth-century readership, and no other known example of his work being translated. As well as providing texts of Chatwin's versions, this article sets out what little is known of their author, and considers his interest in the poems at a time when, according to the widely received view, 'there was no demand for Henry Vaughan'.[1] Taking hints from the translations themselves and from other poems in manuscript, it suggests that Vaughan was known to Chatwin (and perhaps others) not as a great devotional writer, but rather as a forerunner of the classicizing translator-poets of the 1680s whom Chatwin greatly admired – men like Dryden and John Oldham.[2] On this view, Vaughan's appeal to the later seventeenth century, such as it was, may have hinged less on his discipleship of Herbert than on his resemblance to writers such as Cowley or the Neo-Latin poet Casimir Sarbiewski, whose work was translated both by Vaughan (in *Olor Iscanus*) and by Chatwin. In conclusion, it suggests that Chatwin's manuscript may also open the way to further discoveries concerning Vaughan's contemporary readership, centring on the circles of literary exchange in Chatwin's native county of Leicestershire.

---

1 Paul Hammond, 'The Restoration Poetic and Dramatic Canon', in *The Cambridge History of the Book in Britain, IV: 1557-1697*, ed. by John Barnard and D. F. McKenzie (Cambridge: Cambridge University Press, 2002), p. 390.

2 On Dryden and Oldham, see Bodleian MS Rawl. poet. 94 (Chatwin's manuscript miscellany), pp. 149-50, and pp. 156-8. Subsequent references to Chatwin's poems will be given in parentheses in the text.

Chatwin's translations of Vaughan occur about two thirds of the way through the written portion of his manuscript, on pages 183-5[3]:

Ad Fluviam Iscam, paraphrastically translated out of Master Vaughan's poems

> Isca, whose fruitfull Streams make flowers rise,
>   And with thy frothy Lips dost kiss
> Pebbles more glorious than the Spangled Skies.
> Who by thy dewy whispers keep'st alive,
>   And mak'st Sad Hyacinth revive,   [5]
> And all thy Sandy painted Glories thrive.
> Thou, whilst the hasty Months do Swiftly fly,
> Which new officious Moons with Light Supply,
>   And Heav'n consumes Mortality,
> Dost hoard up dayes with the bright frugal Sun,   [10]
> So with like vigour dost thro' thousand Ages run.
> Thou dost the Groves with gliding murmurs please,
> With all the num'rous throng of list'ning Trees.
> Thro' thee the mangled Thracian's sad complaint,
>   And all his pensive Musick went.   [15]

Ad Echum. out of the same

> O Nymph! who thro' the Shady Woods dost fly,
> Thro' dark Recesses, and Obscurity,
> And mak'st thy pratling voice Still multiply.
> Thou pleasant Genius of the aged Shades,
> Thou Oracle of those cool awfull Beds!   [5]
> Whom our last dying Accents only please,
> And Thou t'each Grove dost bear them by degrees.
> By Thee Narcissus's latest words I'd hear,
> Th'unhappy beauteous Boy's dissolving pray'r;
> His last Essayes of Life I fain would know,   [10]
> And the deep Sighs that from his mouth did flow.
> Grant I these uncouth paths of Woods may Shew,
> And all their Grots and Secret Windings view;
> So these green Shades luxurious Gifts Shall bring,
> Blest with a glorious and eternall spring;   [15]

---

3 The spelling, punctuation, and lineation of the manuscript have been preserved; underlining indicates expansion of a scribal contraction.

And thy fresh Bow'rs each Night Shall tast alone
The virgin tears of the Balsamick moon;
Heav'n's sweetest Dew Shall on their branches lie,
And it's warm breathings thro' the leaves Shall fly.
When wasted Stars shall from their orbs drop down,   [20]
Perpetuall youth their Smiling heads Shall crown;
A constant vigour Shall their Roots Supply,
Till with the rowling Spheres their Age may vie!
So may they Gumms, perfumes, and Spices Spread,
Such as the Phoenix in her fun'rall Bed;   [25]
Or those that from *Panchaia's* cloudy flames are bred.

The miscellany containing these poems is now held in the Bodleian Library as part of the literary collection within the Rawlinson manuscripts, shelf mark Rawlinson poet. 94. A bound quarto book of 350 pages, it contains 147 original poems and translations copied out in Chatwin's hand, an attractive late seventeenth-century italic mixed only in that it also uses the older secretary form of minuscule 'e'. In its range of genres, it recalls earlier seventeenth-century university miscellanies: pastoral dialogues and love verses are mingled with Horatian meditations on the attractions of retirement and country life; translations of classical Latin poetry – and less often Neo-Latin, as in the case of Vaughan – flow into squibs on student life, which in turn give way to verse epistles addressed to friends and patrons. As was common for undergraduates at that time, Chatwin also wrote verses about events of national importance. His celebration of the marriage of Princess Ann and Prince George of Denmark appeared in the tribute volume *Hymnenaus Cantabrigiensis* (Cambridge, 1683), his only printed poem. But MS Rawlinson poet. 94 provides considerable evidence that Chatwin's verse was 'published' in other senses. Its contents are fair copies of poems that would previously have circulated in manuscript, both among their intended recipients in the case of verse letters, and more widely within the social circles in which Chatwin moved at Cambridge and in his native Leicestershire. The book itself may also have been intended for circulation, since it includes a long and meticulous index ('A TABLE') at the rear of the book, and a modest title page ('POEMS') at the front. Writing about the continuing importance of manuscript culture in the seventeenth century, Margaret Ezell has seen these features of Chatwin's manuscript as striking evidence for the practice of 'social authorship': the circulation of poetry among friends and patrons in manuscript as a way for an individual to 'respond to what he read and to comment on the significant public events of his day, both locally and nationally' outside of the growing commercial marketplace of print.[4]

4 Margaret Ezell, *Social Authorship and the Advent of Print* (Baltimore: Johns Hopkins University Press, 1999), p. 33.

Despite clear generic continuities with earlier seventeenth-century miscellanies, Chatwin's book is also evidently a Restoration compilation. This is seen, for instance, in topical subjects such as libertinism and drunkenness, the nature of male friendship, and the evolving role of poetry and the arts – the latter seen particularly in Chatwin's praise of those who have 'retrieved' writing for a new age, notably Aphra Behn (p.50), Anne Killigrew (pp. 149-52) and John Oldham ('In the Praise of Poetry', p. 156). Stylistically, too, Chatwin is a child of his times: he works almost exclusively in the heroic couplet form as it had been developed by Waller, Dryden, and others, or else writes odes influenced by Cowley and Dryden. Chatwin's translations of Vaughan are written in rhyming couplets, but 'Ad Fluviam Iscam' varies pentameter with tetrameter lines, producing something of the effect of Vaughan's alternating hexameter and iambic dimeter.[5] On the rare occasions Chatwin deserts the iamb, his rhythmical dexterity recalls that of Jonson and the Caroline lyricists. One of his imitations of Catullus, for instance, is written in bounding anapaests: 'Come, come my Orinda and now let us prove / The Secret enioyments of innocent Love' ('Song', p. 121). Typically, though, he returns to iambs for his stricter translation of Catullus's 'Ad Lesbiam': 'Dear Lesbia, let us love and play, / Not caring what Old Age can say' (p. 191).

While Vaughan's presence in Chatwin's book is obviously unusual for its time, other texts reveal a more straightforwardly fashionable literary taste. The texts Chatwin chooses from Petronius Arbiter and Catullus, for instance, also crop up in *A Miscellany of Poems by Oxford Hands* (Oxford, 1685), as do five poems by Anacreon that Chatwin also chose. Anacreon's songs of wine and friendship had been favoured by Civil War era poets such as Lovelace, Stanley, and Cowley, but were also newly fashionable in the 1680s following the Earl of Rochester's imitation 'Drinking A Bowl', and John Oldham's versions in *Poems and Translations* (1683). *Anacreon done into English* (Oxford, 1683) was published by the same bookseller as *Oxford Hands*, and featured work by Cowley, Oldham, and others. The similarity between Chatwin's choices and these new classical anthologies suggests an awareness on the young man's part of the emerging classical repertoire that was fuelling what one critic has called the 'golden age of poetic translation'.[6] Also fashionable again in the 1680s was the Polish Jesuit Casimir Sarbiewski, two of whose poems—'Ad Cicadem' and 'Ad Rosam'—Chatwin translates (they are also in *Oxford Hands*). A new edition of Casimir's verse was published in Cambridge in 1684, but it is possible that

5 John T. Shawcross, 'Neo-Latin Poetry and Henry Vaughan', in *Intentionality and the New Traditionalism: Some Liminal Means to Literary Revisionism* (University Park, PA: Pennsylvania University Press, 1991), pp. 131-40 (p. 135).

6 Paul Davis, *Translation and the Poet's Life* (Oxford: Oxford University Press, 2008), p. 2.

Chatwin had already sought out earlier editions after reading Vaughan's translations in *Olor Iscanus* (itself reissued in 1679).[7] Casimir is in fact the only Neo-Latin author chosen by Chatwin more times than Vaughan: the others in his book, the Caroline poet Thomas Randolph and the sixteenth-century humanist George Buchanan, feature only once (pp. 141-2, 279). Casimir's own popularity in England had been growing since the 1630s and culminated with George Hils's complete translation of the Odes and poems in 1646.[8]

The new literary culture of translation in the Restoration seems, therefore, to have been partly responsible for Chatwin's attraction to Vaughan. This interest in new English versions of classical texts originated with writers such as Cowley, Thomas Stanley, and of course Vaughan himself, all of whom had begun translating in earnest in the later 1640s and into the 1650s. Recent studies have skilfully explored some of the ways in which Vaughan's translation from Ovid, Boethius, Ausonius, and Casimir in *Olor Iscanus* constituted a search for poetic and political identity following the personal and cultural trauma of the English Civil Wars.[9] While John Chatwin may not have had such urgent cause for literary self-seeking, he seems to have been drawn to those poems of Vaughan's in which the figure of the poet is delineated by means of classical myth and literature. 'Ad Echum', for instance, derives from *Metamorphoses* Book 3, though also drawing more widely on classical associations between Echo and the Muses in its vision of her as '*Annosi* numen *nemoris*' ('deity of the age-old forest').[10] 'Ad Fluvium Iscam', too, alludes briefly to the fate of Hyacinthus, and ends with a powerful allusion to the story of Orpheus in *Metamorphoses* Books 10 and 11.

Comparing Chatwin's version of 'Ad Fluviam Iscam' with the original from *Olor Iscanus*, it is possible to sense the younger poet encountering Vaughan

---

7 This was the Latin-only edition *Mathiae Casimiri Sarbievii Lyricorum* (Cambridge: Richard Green, 1684).

8 *The Odes of Casimire* (London: for Humphrey Moseley, 1646). On Sarbiewski see George Gömöri, '"The Polish Swan Triumphant": The English Reception of Maciej Kazimierz Sarbiewski in the Seventeenth Century', *Modern Language Review*, 106 (2011), 814-33; *Casimir Britannicus: English Translations, Paraphrases, and Emulations of the Poetry of Maciej Kazimierz Sarbiewski*, ed. by Krzysztof Fordoński and Piotr Urbański, expanded edn (London: MHRA, 2010); and Maren-Sofie Røstvig, 'Casimire Sarbiewski and the English Ode', *Studies in Philology*, 51 (1954), 443-60.

9 Robert Wilcher, '"Feathering some slower hours": Henry Vaughan's Verse Translations', *Scintilla* 4 (2004), 142-161; Peter Thomas, 'Henry Vaughan, Orpheus, and the Empowerment of Poetry', in *Of Paradise and Light: Essays on Henry Vaughan and John Milton in Honor of Alan Rudrum*, ed. by Donald R. Dickson and Holly Faith Nelson (Newark: University of Delaware Press, 2004), pp. 218-249; Davis, pp. 40-74.

10 Discussed by Davis on pp. 52, 57; cf. Joseph Loewenstein, *Responsive Readings: Versions of Echo in Pastoral, Epic, and the Jonsonian Masque* (New Haven: Yale University Press, 1984).

through the Ovidian myth of Orpheus familiar to him from his schoolboy Latin:

Ad Fluviam Iscam

Isca parens florum, placido qui spumeus ore
    Lambis lapillos aureos,
Qui maestos hyacinthos, et picti ανθεα tophi
    Mulces susurris humidis,
Dumque novas pergunt menses consumere lunas   [5]
    Coelumque mortales terit,
Accumulas cum sole dies, aevumque per omne
    Fidelis induras latex,
O quis inaccessos et quali murmure lucos
    Mutumque solaris nemus!   [10]
Per te discerpti credo Thracis ire querelas
    Plectrumque divini senis.[11]

The key to Chatwin's Ovidian interpretation lies in the way nature is animated in his translation. Whereas in the original the woods and remote groves ('inaccessos . . . lucos', l. 9) are dumb or silent ('mutum', l. 10) in response to the consoling power of the Usk, in Chatwin's version the groves and trees are said to be 'list'ning' with pleasure to the river's 'gliding murmurs'. The rustling, leafy onomatopoeia of 'list'ning' transforms the trees into more active partic-ipants in the scene; and in so doing they strengthen and anticipate the refer-ences to the 'divine old man' Orpheus, among whose powers was the ability to make 'Beasts, Trees, and Stones' respond, and even move, through the force of his song.[12] Book 10 of the *Metamorphoses* relates how Orpheus' tuning of his lyre brings trees to shade him from the burning sun, after which 'the Poet' is able to sing his songs, 'though dissonant, yet musicall', which include that of the doomed youth Hyacinthus.[13] This moment is also remembered in Chatwin's poem 'In the Praise of Poetry', which tells how 'The Ancient Trees their Native Soyle forsook, / With Musick ravish'd, and amazement Struck' (ll. 17-18, p. 156). The hint of extra animation in the trees of 'Ad Fluvium Iscam' suggests that Chatwin is seeing the poem through the lens of this Ovidian moment.

---

11 *Henry Vaughan: The Complete Poems*, ed. by Alan Rudrum, revised edn (Harmondsworth: Penguin, 1983), p. 130. Subsequent references to Vaughan's poems are given in the text.
12 George Sandys, *Ovid's Metamorphoses Englished, Mythologized, and Represented in Figures* [1632], ed. by Karl K. Hulley and Stanley T. Vandersall (Lincoln, NE: University of Nebraska Press, 1970), XI.2 (p. 497).
13 Sandys, X.146-7 (p.457).

Thus his translation accents what in Vaughan is remembered much more mutedly: the power of Orpheus's song over nature itself.

By emphasizing the river's harmony with mankind, Chatwin's translation changes the way the Usk is seen to influence its surroundings. For Vaughan the river is a source of comfort and appeasement ('mulces', l. 4, 'solaris', l. 10), whose waters spring calmly ('placido . . . ore', l. 1) to soothe the flora with 'moist whispers' ('susurris humidis', l. 4). Its 'unfailing stream' ('Fidelis . . . latex', l. 8) strengthens the poet to hold firm in the 'credo' of line 11 to a belief that, as Peter Thomas has written, 'all the tears shed in *Olor* are absorbed (and redeemed) in that comforting Orphic whisper along Usk in which the voice of nature and the voice of indestructible song are one'.[14] In Chatwin, the 'credo' of the poem is removed, and the consoling power of nature seems to flow instead from a more easily asserted equivalence between the ways of man and those of nature, a fundamentally pastoral idea. The lapping motion of the Usk's waters ('lambis', l.2) is transformed into the 'kiss' of nature, the river's foaming source becoming its 'frothy Lips'. This mother Nature or goddess of the groves is more human in her actions and in her consolations; the poem she presides over sees man and nature as fitting together into a whole more easily than the original from which it is derived. By comparison, Vaughan's poem finds succour and consolation in the Usk, but its 'credo' speaks of the faith required to achieve this in the face of the suffering and uncertainty recorded elsewhere in *Olor Iscanus*.

Yet if Chatwin is reading Vaughan partly through the lens of Ovidian epic or classical pastoral, he is also surely responding both to the mood of *Olor* and to the language and style of its author. His 'dewy whispers' (l. 4) recall Vaughan's 'spicy whispers' from 'To the River Isca' (l. 64) and may also be influenced by the many images of dew used by Vaughan throughout his writing: 'dew' and 'dewy' appear thirty-five times in his poetry alone, the most remarkable concentration being that of the expanded *Silex Scintillans*, with a total of twenty-three uses.[15] The Silurist's fascination with dew shows in such punning lines as those from 'Retirement' in which 'the *Dove* / Duly as *dew*, comes from above' (ll. 25-6), or the moment in 'The Bee' when wild flowers in the woods have 'rich, unrifled *Sweets* [which] | With a chaste kiss the cool dew greets' (ll. 25-6). Kissing and dew together, then – Chatwin's pastoral mode of translating the Usk – are far from alien to Vaughan's poetic language. In 'To the River Isca', too, kissing and *whispering* are found together when Vaughan writes how

---

14 Thomas, p. 235.

15 Vaughan uses 'dew' twenty-one times and 'dewy' twice. Statistics from Imelda Tuttle, *Concordance to Vaughan's 'Silex Scintillans'* (University Park: Pennsylvania State University Press, 1969), p. 49, and searches of the Chadwyck Healey *English Poetry* database.

'*roses* shall *kiss*' while the '*spicy whispers*' blow round (ll. 60, 64), while the poem's closing wish is that that '*freedom, safety, joy, and bliss*' should be '*United* in one loving *kiss*' (ll. 83-4). As well as the possibility of Vaughan's direct influence on Chatwin, what this congruence of language also highlights is the shared classical literary heritage of the two poets.

Shortly after he compiled his miscellany, Chatwin 'vanished from record', leaving no further record of his engagement with Vaughan's poetry.[16] However, one further biographical clue within his poems provides an additional explanation for how it was that he came to read Vaughan at a time when he was by and large neglected. The only poem clearly not by Chatwin is 'The Witch of Endor' (pp. 185-8), a narrative poem by the Coventry clergyman-poet Nathaniel Wanley (1632/3-80), whose body of sacred verse from the 1650s and 60s, *Scintillulae Sacrae*, are clearly imitative of Henry Vaughan. It is not clear that Chatwin and Wanley ever met, but both were natives of Leicestershire and moved in overlapping circles. Wanley's first ecclesiastical living after the Restoration was Chatwin's home town of Lutterworth, a post he obtained through the patronage of the previous incumbent, Thomas Pestell, himself a poet of some reputation.[17] With Wanley and other poet-clergy like Wanley's mentor John Bryan, Pestell belonged to literary coteries in the counties of Leicestershire and Warwickshire, within which poems were circulated and ideas shared about the role of poetry within the ministry. Wanley's preferred mode was the short religious lyric modelled on George Herbert, whose *The Temple* had become something of a calling card for moderate godly ministers in the mid-seventeenth century.[18] But it is clear from several touches in his poems that Wanley has also read Vaughan's *Silex Scintillans*, and although Chatwin praises Wanley's narrative verse rather than his sacred lyrics, the connection is too strong for Chatwin's reading of Vaughan to be entirely coincidental. Further work on the circles in which Chatwin, Vaughan, Pestell, and Bryan moved may yet reveal additional evidence for the reading, imitating, and translating of Vaughan's poetry in Interregnum and Restoration Leicestershire.

---

16 Ezell, p. 31.

17 Biographical information on Wanley is taken from Philip West, 'Wanley, Nathaniel (1632/3-1680)', *Oxford Dictionary of National Biography* (Oxford: Oxford University Press, 2004); *The Poems of Thomas Pestell*, ed. by Hannah Buchan (Oxford: Blackwell, 1940).

18 Philip West, 'Nathaniel Wanley and George Herbert: The Dis-Engaged and *The Temple*', *Review of English Studies*, 57 (2006), 337-58.

Emiko Aida, *Sailing*

HOWARD WRIGHT

Heatwave

Rolls over the trolley parked with a shoe and brown bottles
in the lay-by, its blunt ribcage snapped against the glare:
someone is down a pound. And the boy bouncing a ball
is looking for a match going on somewhere; over there
with the yells, kicks and falling over, the letting go
on unmarked pitches. What goes around comes around.
It breaks over the mother and child, not taking their eyes off
each another, pram-pushing huggermugger, riding the surf
to sleep and melt together while horses stand up to their necks
in the haze. They watch the world, their bucket, fill with dust.
And outside that rusted pail, the turned field is stabbed
with builders' crosses to the death of nature, the first phase,
and the tricycle squatting at a privet hedge is consumed
and spat out along a path cut through ragged weeds
to grassless housing, just cooled, union jacks at full mast,
full tilt, celebrating now England are again out
of the competition, having won a few keenly sarcastic cheers.
It crashes there and leaves deep pools of peace in its wake,
a plastic bag wavering with all the mendacity of a white cat.

The Repair Kit

To see your life in the failure of others – dogma, orthodoxy,
mock teenage-soap philosophy, sensitive and trite –
means you too have exhausted the need to find a reason
when, far from your door, a nail or upright tack, an arrowhead

of glass, breaks the defences and you grind the metal rim,
making it a long walk home where the frame is upturned
for a cold clutch of dessert spoons and the wheel set to spin

above a basin of warm water and gasping pump, the kind
fitting snug to your greasy palm. Next, from the garage, a kit
of sandpaper, glue, chalk-cube and round foil-backed plasters;
the tyre duly gutted and gouged and inner tube dipped

for the welcome sight of bubbles and healed with heavy thumbs,
to be re-chained and freed over the pleasant click of pedals,
the inflated tread lightly catching your barely-working fingers.

The Old School

The patched pool table clicks its fingers with impatience,
squat as a sultan. The news is delivered in subtitles
following the curve of the sky at the top of the world,

a slashed New York canvas. Something is going on everywhere:
tanks and wide-eyed brutality, chanting and a show of force;
the world falling through a hole in the night's fabric,

the evening star pointing out the woman asleep upstairs.
She forms a swastika directly above our heads, the bar where
across two walls is pinned the history of paper money – dollars,

francs and marks, billions in used profiles. Behind us, a mirror
and the image of the barmaid in less modern perspectives:
Manet adored her, Degas brushed the gleam of her shoulder,

and naughty Lautrec lifted her foaming skirts. The old school
knew what it was doing. They too watched sunsets embrace
all beauty's face and the unrelenting violence of life.

CHRIS PREDDLE

Somme

Somme the River God, angry in his hoops,
rose and ran over, in under the heaps
of the dead. O Meuse and Simoïs, Oise and Shatt al-Arab,
be a burial-sheet
for humans humans discarded; Amu River,
discover her, cover her.
Each was in someone's mind – an afterlife
he might be sure of. Whom sun and mind have left,
no makers making,
kiss, clip and clear them away, Thames, Potomac and Mekong.

Tianfei

Girl
cramoysin on the harbour-bar, be to us
Tianfei, sea-goddess of the treasure fleet.
Seamark, seaguide us to Malacca, Kollam,
Ormuz, Malindi, to the sea's uttermost
mark and margin. Twenty kings compelled
complied. We brought the west into the order
All Under Heaven, as a mariner
brought cramoisi to the seagirl Lin Moniang.

Sappho

'What is it, Sappho,
you suffer now,' my goddess asked, 'so far

into the future?' I answered, 'Scholars keep asking and asking
about lacunae in my poem of Tithonus aging,

lagoons or gaps in the papyrus beds. Whatever belongs
in the vacancy, I've quite forgotten – I live so long

through the iniquity of time.
Quit me, time.

My arms are paperwhite on the bed. I am papery thin as
Tithonus.

But whenever you, my goddess Dawn,
like a wife come down to me, your rose-red clothes undone,

I am like you goddess immortal,
as those gappy papyrus poems of mine may tell.'

Tethys

Tethys rose out of the sea for him
as he walked away silenced along the beach. 'I am the Tethys Ocean.
You're one of the all-at-a-loss, for whom

I broke up All-Earth or C-shaped Pangaea,
and pushed away Gondwana from Laurasia. They broke apart with seacries
who had been joined.

You might, I suppose, be Chryses
the priest of Apollo, or the youth who sat on the rocks one summer,
or any Chris in a crisis.

I brought the continent Cimmeria
that you might sit here. I made this southern coast
that you might mourn in Europe. I too may seem

diminished, to this Mid-Earth Sea. All-human, accost
the shingle god and sea's aggriever whom
the waves accuse, whom they break themselves against.'

REGINA WALTON

Looking at Memling

Today he does not want to read *The Runaway Bunny*
Or *Blueberries for Sal*, but drags over
The heavy art book with the sloe-eyed
Angel on the cover.
He sits in my lap as we flip past
Three-quarter profiles of men with pageboys and embroidered collars
Until we arrive at the mother lode –
Painting after painting of the Madonna and Child.

He is delighted that Jesus, like him, is strawberry-blond
And round-bellied, leaning in to nurse
From a pale, grapefruit-sized orb
Protruding from the yards and yards
Of the BVM's drapery.
But the proportions are off – the long-awaited one
Is neither baby nor child,
More like a homunculus, who could,
After suckling, raise an elfin finger
And start sorting sheep from goats then and there.
Mary, amid her shining tresses and upholstery,
Wears the same languid expression in each pose.

We pause at one picture
With a dollhouse castle in the upper-right hand corner.
He asks if Jesus will go inside it.
Yes, I say, and suddenly I imagine
The Mother of God snapping awake and climbing off her throne,
Dragging her voluminous folds behind her,
Turning while she still can –
Pulling away from the gaggle of prophets,
Scaling the slope towards the shelter
With the babe on her hip,
Around her neck his tiny, unmarked hands.

ROBERT NISBET

Hotel Room, Bermuda

*Dark'n'Stormy, often regarded as Bermuda's national drink, is made of rum,
lime juice, Angostura bitters and ginger beer.*

The room had the humid grace
of the Southern USA, maybe it was
the veranda opening to the trees outside.
In the heat we'd passed the four o'clock drink,
iced tea, and now, sensing evening's pull,
turned to Dark'n'Stormy, cold fiery island draught.
The tree frogs now were booming into voice.

Reading, we looked at the London papers,
two days old, brought down from the airport.
There were riots in Tottenham, knives, cries of hate.
Unbelieving, we looked at pictures
of black skies wild with fire . . .

. . . as the sky outside plunged almost at once
to a deep dark. The trees sweltered, the frogs' croak
was swelling now, nature's bass note,
nature's black root.

As You Like It in the Bishop's Palace

An open-air production in St. David's

A coastal summer and cathedral bells
and the rooks' hauteur give us this night in Bardic country.
Foreground, romance in a forest.

From the back row of canvas chairs
they watch, they two.
They have not yet adventured.
But the voice of the lovers is reaching them
from the forest, from the palace,
and as eight o'clock deepens to a cooler nine
they draw the blanket more around themselves,
nestle.

Rosalind and Orlando are eighteen, nineteen,
but grown to love's confidence
in the play's disguise.
The playwright stakes out his promise:
Hang there, my verse, in witness of my love.

The watching two are in thrall.
Their hands, beneath the blanket,
steal together, clasp,
as in the happy ending of a play.

CHRIS NORRIS

from Symbolon: An Essay on Rhyme

One half of some big truth is what they tell,
    The poets – one side only of some twin-
Faced spheric *symbolon* whose fractured shell
    Might yet take on an oscillating spin
And so, by hysteresis, work to quell
    Our zeal for that big truth. It may begin
As pure conjecture and so let us dwell
    On flipside options, but then have us pin

Our bets on the front-runner and expel
    To mere oblivion all the might-have-been
Alternatives whose Bayesian quotient fell
    Below the figure reckoned fit to win
The truth-stakes. One technique to break the spell
    Of certitude is that which lies within
The rhymester's gift: to show how words rebel
    Against the rules that stipulate what's kin

To what by strict enforcement of the claim
    To conjugate in ways that make good sense
By spurning rhyme's seductions with the same
    Strict vigilance as springs to the defence
Of all those mine-strewn boundaries that frame
    Our sexual like our verbal couplings. Whence,
One might surmise, the curious taint of shame
    Or odd capacity to give offence

(Think Wittgenstein) in any language-game
    That opts to 'go on holiday', dispense
With ordinary usage, junk the aim
    Of communal accord, and thus commence
On wayward paths. These tempt us, in the name
    Of verbal art, so tightly to condense
The gist or (now think Jakobson) untame
    Rhyme's latent chaosmos at the expense

Of common parlance as to leave small room
    For those proprieties that custom might
Commend to our best selves or law presume
    To lay down in its will to reunite
The cultural with the natural and so groom
    Us up in strict accord with what's deemed right
In love and language. So who pairs with whom,
    And does so legally, is within sight

Of other questions like why critics fume
    So much (or anyway the more uptight
Amongst them) when they hear a rhyme-word loom
    Despite the regnant veto, and take fright
As if it presages some Poe-type doom
    Or catastrophic gender/*genre* blight
Let loose by any effort to exhume
    The noisome corpse of rhyme and so invite

The kind of bad come-uppance that awaits
    Such ventures in a necrophiliac vein
That flout what modern decency mandates.
    And so the word-health warning goes: abstain
From any verse-craft that resuscitates
    Old tricks like rhyme just as you'd best refrain,
So far as sexual rectitude equates
    With formal etiquette, from that old bane

Of kindred-love that kicks in when the mates
    We first select and shared delights we gain
By consanguinity are what the fates
    Then use to plague us, whether through a strain
Of botched gene-replication that dictates
    Worse ills to come, or else more in the vein
Of Oedipal disaster that creates
    Unending woe for lovers too germane.

JOCK STEIN

On the Runway

Crane fly challenging the breeze
alights, a tiny airship
on a paper runway. Six knees

genuflect upon a waiting clip
board, asking us to look
beyond a random insect trip

to what is stirring in the book
of Scotland's history, which we
are writing, questioning this fluke

of time which lets us see
so many possibilities, behind
September's serious apogee

of yes or no. I find
this fragile daddy longlegs
focuses the national mind

which flits between the dregs
of fear and sheer mis-selling
of the arguments. It begs

the issue, which is spelling
out in song and story who we are
and want to be: not telling

one another we'll be far
more wealthy if we choose
this way or that. The bar

must rise, so that we lose
our fatal lust for things
that rust and die, refuse

the lies, hold truth which brings
us hope, and trust that sees
our lift off come on gentle wings.

ALAN PAYNE

North

for Roger Hubank

No longer able to bound down screes
after a steep ascent; often out of breath;
he's preparing, still, for the trek –
crampons in the hall, ice-pick in his van.

No taste for food. But a bottle of wine
on a table reminds him of friends.
His books near-by: *Hazard's Way,*
Taking Leave, Evening Light.

In his pocket, a stone from the Alps,
a photo of his daughter's confirmation;
and in his mouth, the shock of scooped water
on his last journey to the north.

That They Are There!

for Roger Hubank,
from 'Psalm' by George Oppen

Not only the deer, startled, staring out,
but geese, in flight, low in the sky,

seals, bobbing, with inquisitive eyes,
seen from the Emblestones,

and further north, near Lindisfarne,
terns, eider ducks, cormorants,

messengers from beyond the cabins
perched above the dunes

where a man might reflect on a psalm,
or on the Black Cuillin

where once he climbed, and remember
moments of joy, as well as doubt,

and watch, lit by a rare light,
clouds like a succession of white ships.

THOMAS R. SMITH

Holy Saturday

1.
End of March, snow finally in retreat.
The cold lifts its leather glove from our heart.
In the Glen shadowy ice still
hangs in dirty tatters like grey felt.
The river's horses will carry it away.

2.
Today we heard, then saw, the first robin
on the tallest branch, high in sun, making
its small tribute to spring's river of song.
Easter Sunday is almost here. I wrap
the warm throw of mystery around my shoulders.

3.
I don't want to look back and wonder
where I was when my life was happening.
So many moments pass unnoticed.
For the sake of silence, I keep the market-
place at a distance on holy days.

4.
We've forgotten the old stories in which
we gave up something to consciously
partake in the sacrifice. What's the
sacrifice? This little death we practice together
to make the rivers rise again singing.

CHARLES WILKINSON

Caves

ancestral sleepers
in a circle: feet towards the fire's
red tongue – warming a dormitory of stone
cut into a mountain's head; first furniture
   hewn from rock; the mouth-roof dripped water
   thoughts; dreams were unfathomable,
     older than Arthur

later the thin-flamed
candles found a hand-axe & bones of
beasts & men; burins & bracelets; faces
of animals carved on a rib from the feast;
   – reindeer drawn on walls; there were legends
   of lakes – & treasures that lay
     behind waterfalls

the skulls of early
home – & profit, where the veins' glitter
was worked deeper; matter's neural seams connect
desire for black & gold; tales left in the caves
   with the sleepers or lost in language:
   a tongue thick with earth & over
     which a stone has rolled.

who can find the field
where the hazel was cut or know one
moment before print when words' entranced naming
exacted springs from rock? the old utterances long-
   stopped: backed by an echo or shadows falling
   from outside substance in ancient
     sunlit afterglow

from 'Of the Red & the White Books'

Maxen

lady in a gold chair
waits in an Emperor's dream

      castle & mountains a white peak
      the broad-mouthed river
                 two boys
      who do not speak play a game
      on a silver board
            an old man
      in a seat of ivory
            carves a figure

in flaxen heat
      Lord of the west (Maxen)
his visions as real as the jugs
on the table
      praxis – the unity
      of dream & world

his messengers track traces
prove real the myths of sleep

          find the river the towers a castle
        & keep the boys with the auburn hair
          an old man carving & the lady alive
        in the red gold chair
vision as theory
in Imperial action

night-thoughts of the great
lend weight to wraiths
      dragged from dream
      into conquest
the legend of the pure voice
winning a small country

the customs of malpratice
    engagement as a taste
of the blood reverie

    murder the men-folk
    cut out the tongues of women
a mix of race is allowed yet
language must not be blent

speak with the original proud lilt
in Llydaw land of the half silent

MARGARET WILMOT

IS

1.

Stepping out onto the quay before dawn
in a biting wind
to see
what I may see
    the tide is
    coming in
    a huge dark
    rush and
    thrust
    there is
    that slap, that physical
    push
    so close below this wooden platform
    (no rail)
    the all-night quay-lights
    die on that
    dark glint and swallow
    that skin of matter's
    utter authority
    the verb *is*
    for me, cold awe
    which makes my gut go taut

2.

How clear-cut the mountains
stand against a pale flush of sky. Mist rolls
through the cleft, thick grey, unfurls
into the high bowl of heath.
A rim of sun pushes at
cloud heaped in strata on the sea.

New Year's Day, and the world does feel new.
The cows on fodder in their barns, and me
ruminating: relative to my years
on earth the days here so few.

On the edge
of an old sea-bed spongy under juniper
we found flint chips – some ancient settlement.
In this new place I saw my husband's face
tilt up
         listening
and shine
as a curlew chirred.

3.

The hotel-room doors were glass.
We stepped out of bed onto moor-land
where in the early light
the tussocks and hummocks
became grazing sheep-backs.
Lichens and mosses emerged,
stained outcrops of rock
salmon, and ochre. A ridge of hills
showed low in the east.

We walked a while – our feet
soon wet – saw mountains to the north.
Turning back, we couldn't tell
which door was ours.

4.

Two peaks align into pyramids.
Cheops? Khephren? I sketch the air.
They travel with you, the dead. Alive,
Mother never came so far north, but here she is
on this rough track, and we're talking Egypt

again. I mention a memoir I read
from the Fifties, when we were there.
Her laugh makes little waves in a pocket of air.
Chunks of ice creak as we pass a small bay.
The sun is an orange ball rolling
along the low coastal range.

5.

Where did we first know
the authority of matter?
Lichen grooved rock

                This cloud, which even now
           I long to climb

Three-years old holding
my mother's hand instructed expressly
that's water – and I could see
the pool tremble beneath its green algal mat
rich as a carpet –
still
the foot stepped

On a river-walk
       (sixteen? twenty-three?)
passing a deep pool
came that tug –

       fully clothed
             I dived

6.

Earlier we strolled up to the bridge, stood looking
at boats perched over mirror-selves.
Dad marvelled. *Nothing blocks the view.*

It's rare for him to visit me in dreams.
*Remember my cataract op? How fresh the world
seemed after?* I pour us each a scotch.

He starts telling what happens to colours
when you die. *They come alive, 3-D, bleed
with their own sap, speak, play.* He laughs,

and his beard's gone black again.
*Alizarin is a cool number. Cobalt flashes a leg.
Gamboge grabs my brush, paints day.*

7.

I've strayed on the heath,
and an arm of water
breaks across my way.
I climb up through juniper
onto a huge lump
of granite, grooved,
water-smoothed –
from some pre-Atlantic ocean?
They say this edge of the island
was America, before
America was –
and stand looking for
the path, lost somewhere
among the hummocks
and hollows. Looking
without concern,
a child with all the day
to play, no purpose
beyond being,
and being here.

Emiko Aida, *Warm kitty*

ABSENCE, PRESENCE:
Recalling Peter Thomas

ANNE CLUYSENAAR

Peter's death brought to its end a conversation which has enriched my life over some twenty years. But, as the days go by, I have been discovering how such dialogues may continue beyond death, so that a voice no longer heard is still perceived – questioning, elaborating, proposing witty alternatives to first thoughts.

An image comes, of our first meeting. On a long corridor of closed doors at Cardiff University, one door was almost always open. As I passed, I would hear low strains of classical music and, attracted by these, would glance in to find walls enlivened with images and texts. One day, stopping long enough to focus on a text blown up and placed over the desk, I read 'the living past, the dying present': words of a poet dear to me, Edward Thomas. At that, I could no longer resist. I knocked on the open door and the conversations began.

'The living past, the dying present' – these thoughts, inscribed by chance on the threshold of our work together, also run like a thread through my most immediate memories. In *Scintilla 19*, dedicated to Peter, there will be opportunities to do justice both to his scholarly insights and to the central role he played not only in the establishment of the Vaughan Association and its yearly Colloquium but also, thanks to his organisational skills and elegant editorship, in the foundation and development of this journal. What he contributed in all these areas has left a continuing presence. However, remembering him at this time, I hope simply to record some sense of what he taught me about the importance, in our world, of the Vaughan legacy.

When we met that day, I had only recently discovered in myself a fascination, I may say an obsession, with Henry Vaughan. Neither at ease with religious doctrine nor an ardent Royalist, my overwhelmingly intense response to Vaughan's poems puzzled me, was even something of an embarrassment. Through intermittent discussions with Peter, I began to see that what so drew me in was the poems' experiential depth, questioning intelligence and realism. Even though Vaughan tackles the doctrinal and political issues of his time with honesty and

171

vigour (as Peter has shown in 'The Poisoned Grove')[1] there also flows in his poems a deep tide of life little effected by culture or time. The poems' 'broken stile' alerts a reader to their source in intensely lived moments and in the kind of thought that is a vital part of such moments. In the words of Jimmy Burns Singer, 'thought is always and only thought: / The thinking's different: thinking's in the blood'. Personal honesty combined with intellectual rigour make Henry's voice useful to us in our own world, a world whose true dimensions grow harder and harder to grasp. *Silex Scintillans* still offers, as he hoped it might to his contemporaries, a living body of work 'as useful now in the *publick*, as it has been to me in *private*'.[2] All the better perhaps if reading him enables us to feel on the pulses, to an extent Vaughan himself might not have anticipated, the possibility of deep connection despite political or religious difference.

When Peter chose the usual quotations from Henry and Thomas Vaughan to introduce his first *Scintilla* as General Editor the choices he made were especially significant. From the *Anthroposophia Theomagica* of Thomas, we find this, placed first:

> *Death is 'the recession of life into the unknown', not the*
> *annihilation of any one particle, but a retreat of hidden natures to*
> *the same state they were in before.*

and, to accompany it, these words from Henry's 'They are all gone into the world of light!':

> *So some strange thoughts transcend our wonted themes,*
> *   And into glory peep.*

Reminding myself of this and rereading, in that same issue, Peter's intricate and moving essay 'The Language of Light: Henry Vaughan and the Puritans', I am struck by how convincingly Vaughan is presented there as engaging, especially in *Silex II,* with his times: 'calculatedy argumentative, a tough, combative controversialist, a sophisticated polemicist, an accomplished rhetorician, and a consummate craftsman with designs on his readers . . . As we read we are progressively and firmly brought down to earth, to the natural material things that constitute us, to what "life is"'. Of all Vaughan's poems, one I think Peter particularly admired was 'The Book', for its intelligence and its grasp of the material processes that (in Vaughan's time) went to make a family bible. Con-

---

1 *Scintilla 1*, 1997, p. 27-44.
2 Preface to *Silex Scintillans 1.*

sistent with his argument in that essay, Peter praises the way the poem insists (as does the passage from *Anthroposophia Theomagica*) on 'unbroken process'.[3] To make the Book, matter had in those days to come to life in various forms, die and finally be transformed into material bindings and sacred pages. So a human body comes to be, lives, and is transformed again at death. When Vaughan addresses God in the last verse, the made Book is imagined as an emblem of how all life may be gathered together at the end of time by that 'knowing, glorious spirit':

> O, Knowing, glorious spirit! when
> Thou shalt restore trees, beast and men;
> When thou shalt make all new again,
> Destroying only death and pain,
> Give him amongst thy works a place,
> Who in them lov'd and sought thy face!

One of the texts chosen for the Order of Service at Peter's funeral was 'The Book'. Peter admired, and I think shared, Vaughan's tough practicality, his love of 'fellow creatures' and his honest sense of 'the natural material things that constitute us', but also valued the poet's willingness to acknowledge, despite or because of traumatic times, how 'some strange thoughts transcend our wonted themes'. As Peter wrote in an earlier essay, 'The Poisoned Grove'[4] (where he discusses 'The Book' at some length), 'True poetry, as opposed to feigned utterance,[5] stands revealed as something that takes place where spiritual and material realities intersect and energise one another'.

Whenever Peter's presence comes to me now, it comes in two contrasting, but not contradictory, forms. On one hand, free-flowing phone calls whose exploratory humour never failed to leave me with new insights; on the other, the modestly attentive focus he provided at every Colloquium for those of us who, in some corner of the bar, would sit up talking into the early hours. Both at home and at our future spring meetings I look forward to feeling not only Peter's absence but his presence.

---

3 Scintilla 3, p. 28.
4 *Scintilla 1*, pp. 43-44.
5 We remember Vaughan's account, in 'Anguish', of his struggle to 'write true, unfeigned verse'.

'Into all this':
a tribute to Anne Cluysenaar

FIONA OWEN

'no thing can to Nothing *fall'* – Henry Vaughan,
Resurrection and Immortality

For as long as I have known Anne, she has worn her hair in a bun, pulled back to reveal her face, unadorned, clear and open. It is that face that now smiles gently out from Meic Stephens' obituary, printed in the *Independent*.[1] And I must steel myself to begin using past tense: Anne is someone I *knew*, someone I *loved*.

I met Anne in the late 1990s, at one of the early Usk Valley Vaughan Association colloquia and we *clicked*, as they say. However, it was very easy to *click* with Anne – to admire, respect and love her. I am just one among a great many who have experienced her tragic death[2] with immense shock and sorrow. But, as many of her friends have said, we still have her voice, full of her presence, in her poems and other writings, her body of work. And I know that there is, among many of us, a desire to carry her voice on and out into the world, as poetry that is resonant and relevant, just as it always was.

Along with Peter Thomas, who also sadly died from cancer this autumn,[3] Anne was co-founder of what was then called the Usk Valley Vaughan Association, with its annual journal, *Scintilla*. I have been reading back through past editions, marvelling at what Peter and Anne helped to bring forth. In her preface to the first edition, as general editor, Anne laid out the priorities of the journal, eschewing what she called 'fashionable taboos' that can set 'limits to the scope of thought and of poetry'.[4] Instead, the orientation was to themes 'central to the lives of the Vaughan twins', Henry and Thomas, 'an undeniable,

---

1 http://www.independent.co.uk/news/obituaries/anne-cluysenaar-writer-and-academic-whose-numinous-poetry-drew-on--her-fascination-with-science-as-well-as-her-spirituality-9862395.html.
2 She was killed in her home outside Llantrisant near Usk on Saturday 1st November 2014.
3 September 2014.
4 *Scintilla* 1.

if fleeting, experience of contact, not only with what Henry called "fellow creatures" but with the matter of the universe'. The Vaughans were each, in their own ways, 'driven by a most urgent need to understand the personal and intellectual significance of this ancient human experience' and *Scintilla* would 'provide a meeting-place between writers and readers who, each from their own perspective, experience a similar need'.

I was someone who experienced that similar need back in 1997 when I bought my first copy of *Scintilla*. Little did I know that this would be the beginning of a journey that would lead to Anne, as well as to Peter and all those who have become friends and familiars through the colloquia each April, gatherings I acknowledge as being, for me, formative.

In Anne's preface, I can see *Scintilla* themes that were also her own. She too can be seen, in poem after poem, exploring the 'undeniable, if fleeting, experience of contact' with both 'fellow creatures', human and non-human, and 'the matter of the universe'.

Hers is a poetry of deep attention. A recurring and endearing theme in her work is the sense of care for the past, for the beings that have lived, known to her but also unknown – everyone's ancestors – such as the 'two men and a boy walking at speed' seven thousand years ago 'give or take a few hundred', near the Severn. Their footprints, captured in the silt, are thrown up during a storm in our own time – a moment of human action preserved. They walked 'where they walked, unforeseeing'.[5] In another poem, the narrative voice expresses outrage when 'A newly-discovered cave drawing, dated c.12,000 BP, is attacked': 'O yes, hack them away then, / those traces on rock, like lines / in sand, thinly rough-edged / but precise, gouged out freehand'. For there is 'fellow-feeling there, in the deep / long strokes'.[6] Repeatedly, there is the sense created of commonality between past humans and ourselves, and indeed, the connections between living beings don't stop at the human in Anne's work. There is a moving poem about her cob, Pip, who died in 2012, and here, again, we see her attention to traces:

> It's where he isn't. This dry clod
> fell out of his hoof. And it hasn't yet,
> since he died, been frittered away but lies
> upside down in the field – the precise cast

5 'January 9' in Anne Cluysenaar (2014) *Touching Distances*, Blaenau Ffestiniog, Cinnamon Press, p.28.
6 'September 1' in Anne Cluysenaar (2014) *Touching Distances*, Blaenau Ffestiniog, Cinnamon Press, p.53.

of some step he took, in that gentle way
he had, when here, of being himself.[7]

Reading back through my (precious) email folder entitled 'Anne', there she is, telling me how 'bereft' she was at losing her horse: 'He was such a sweet being. But yesterday I was at least able to write this in his memory'[8] and she sent me the poem.

Reading Anne, you can't help but notice her great sense of empathy for the *creatureliness* of humans and non-humans alike, with *being here* a precious but precarious business. Life-forms can leave traces and it's our human propensity, work of our hands as well as minds, to leave 'precise casts' via such things as poems, paintings, music, cave art, conversations between poets, letters . . . Throughout her poems, there are dedications to other poet-friends, each poem seeming to serve the life of an on-going conversation with, say, Ruth Bidgood or Jeremy Hooker. A letter received, an occasion or conversation shared is catalyst for poem. Quoted lines and phrases help create a rich intertextual weave in Anne's writing, which teems with relationships and a reaching to connect. This is all part of the 'tenuous job of poet' that Anne speaks of in her preface to *Batu-Angas*, her marvellous sequence of twenty four poems where she 'envisions' nature with the nineteenth century natural scientist and co-discoverer of the principle of natural selection, Alfred Russel Wallace. It is 'a multi-millennial meditation' on deep time and the evolutionary drive at the heart of life, where the effect is of languages 'ghost[ing] each other'.[9] This exploratory reach back through time – seeking meaning, understanding but also, crucially, *contact* – is typical of Anne's work.

In an interview I did with Anne about *Batu-Angas*,[10] I asked her how she saw art-making as fitting into evolution. What is 'the tenuous job of poet'? It is to do with survival, she replied, and continuity: 'From deep in prehistory onward, *Homo sapiens* has created art. If art had nothing to do with survival it would not have been given time and attention by people existing on the edge of possibility'. Poets, she said, may (quoting from her final poem in the collection) '"sow the seed of continuance" by helping us recalibrate what goes on in our heads and retain, however much bad news we may know or think we know, a sense of life's wonder'. The arts 'make us want to go on looking and listening, and so help us move on . . .'.

7 'March 26' in Anne Cluysenaar (2014) *Touching Distances*, Blaenau Ffestiniog, Cinnamon Press, p.86.
8 Personal email.
9 Anne Cluysenaar (2008) *Batu-Angas*, Bridgend, Seren.
10 'A New Sense of Balance' – an interview with Anne Cluysenaar in *Planet: the Welsh Internationalist* (December/January 2008/2009).

Anne wrote many poems from the small-holding life near Usk that she shared with her husband for around twenty five years. In all its quotidian detail, there was inevitably a sense of *something more* – a reach for ontological understanding. The exploration of personal memories, fascinating in themselves, also reveal a curiosity (the word etymologically related to 'care') that lies at the heart of one of Anne's key themes, the nature of memory itself – its links with time, imagination, others – and the way lives intersect, inter-relate, inter-connect across time. Synchronicities, dreams and a deeper-down kind of knowing are 'brought up' into poem as if mined from the depths, with threshold experiences connecting the living with the dead.

Reading about Anne's life in her obituary, we can see how much she has achieved in her work and teaching. Yet while her poems display a keen sense of *journeying*, her focus tends to be not so much a literal travelling over surfaces but, rather, a more inward journeying through past, present and imagined future experiences, probing boundaries and wondering at the permeability of selves, so crucially a part of the mystery of being.

Her last two collections are dedicated to her husband of almost forty years, Walt Jackson, and that home, that *oikos*, that shared life comes across as so *dear*: 'For Walt, "to be / just here" she writes in *Migrations* and in her final volume of diary poems, *Touching Distances,* she writes: 'To Walt – "You come safely back. The silent rejoicing of dogs. The stamp of your feet"'.

Anne wrote about death. Like all my favourite poets, she explored this ultimate mystery. Her poetry is full of quickness and this is perhaps because of some kind of deep trust in life's processes. On the loss of her close friend, Michael Srigley, she wrote: 'Your shadow beside me perhaps, in the fold / of a different universe'. In the same poem, she mulled on his thoughts that 'this world might be one in which, / reborn already, we could live yet again'. She likens the page she is working on as it 'darkens with criss and cross – / possibilities, rejections, choices' to the possibility of some kind of parallel existence: 'I see / how the printed page can be only one / of many unprinted but no less real'.[11]

One of my favourite poems by Anne is 'I remember this much. The sun'. When it was first published in *Scintilla*, I remember burbling my praise to her at that year's colloquium. It is one of her epiphany poems, when the mundane seems to dissolve and lose its grip for timeless moments for her to become 'awareness only' before she is returned, with – as she says in a similar poem – a deep experiential sense of being part of something unitive, that 'not one of us / could know, not one escape', something 'Which breathes itself in us':[12]

11 'June 23' in Anne Cluysenaar (2014) *Touching Distances*, Blaenau Ffestiniog, Cinnamon Press, p.49.
12 'There were dark leaves spread out' in Anne Cluysenaar, *Migrations*, Blaenau Ffestiniog, Cinnamon Press, p.95.

I remember this much. The sun
twisting in knots of cloud
down the glacial cwm, one field
then another lit up like reflections
in running water, as if

somewhere behind my back
a world bent down to look
at itself in ours and vanished
into all this – trees, houses,
black-and-white cows grazing –
and whatever I am had become
awareness only.
     I come to
From this to my usual weight,
the scent of grass, a sea-gull
crying its way inland.

Since then, I'm a wave pulled back
from the sea, separated, delighting
in the eye of light at its centre,
the breaking of spume, but willing
to topple whenever into the tide.

Anne knew there was more to the spiritual impulse than religious doctrine and she refused to be confined by any ideas that would put boundaries around her own need to explore and experience the world for herself. She eventually found a spiritual home with Quakers, becoming a member in 2012. She was comfortable with silent worship and the open notion of Inner Light – and in this poem, there is her own insight: 'the eye of light' at the 'centre' of the 'wave pulled back'.

One of the last pieces Anne wrote was her own tribute to Peter Thomas, where she speaks of their 'conversation' over 'some twenty years', and where she discovers 'how such dialogues may continue beyond death, so that a voice no longer heard is still perceived'.

Well, Anne – thank you for letting your life so insightfully speak. I, for one, have been changed for the better by your being among us – and may our dialogues continue in their own ways.

I am so sorry you had to topple in the way you did. But the tide has you now.

13 Published in *Scintilla 18*.

In Memoriam:
Anne Cluysenaar 1936-2014

SUSAN BASSNETT

One of the best known psalms of all is the 23rd, 'The Lord is my shepherd' which is so often used by grieving families at the funeral of loved ones. It is a psalm of hope and strength – the psalmist will fear no evil even in the valley of the shadow of death, because God will comfort him. The last verse is a statement of all that is positive in this world and, for those who believe, in the next: 'But thy loving kindness and mercy shall follow me all the days of my life; and I will dwell in the house of the Lord for ever'.

Psalm 23, significantly, follows on from the darkest of all the psalms , Psalm 22, which opens with the great cry of anguish that is repeated in Matthew's gospel account of the crucifixion: 'My God, My God, why hast thou forsaken me?' It is a psalm I have often gone back to in times of grief, not so much for those words, but rather for the words of verse 14 that provide one of the best descriptions ever written of what grieving feels like:

> I am poured out like water, and all my bones are out of joint:my heart also in the midst of my body is even like melting wax.

The language is that of seventeenth century English, the sentiment is timeless. Whoever first set down those words centuries ago found images to convey the feeling of being suddenly cut off from everyday reality, along with the sense of mind and body dissolving that comes with the shock and then disbelief of losing someone one loves. One's body ceases to function normally, one's heart melts like wax, one's very bones feel dislocated.

I too felt poured out like water, when I heard of the cruel death of my friend of 44 years, Anne Cluysenaar. I had been wondering why she had not replied to my email telling her about plans for a forthcoming visit with my small grandson; then I learned that by the time the email reached her, she was already dead. The message had sped through the ether, never to be read.

Good friendship spans both time and distance. Good friendship endures, grows, changes. Our friendship seemed to deepen as time passed, probably because we shared so much about one another's lives, good and bad, joyous and tragic. I have stayed with her in no less than 5 homes – in Lancaster, Huddersfield, Penistone, Birmingham and finally, Llantrissant in Wales, seen the familiar pieces of furniture, paintings and ornaments rearranged in different spaces. Even in urban surroundings she kept dogs and hens; I remember in one house she bade me listen to the sound of her rabbits, which had reproduced beyond all expectation, tunneling away under the house and expressed anxiety in case the floors gave way. She was not cut out for urban living, so when she finally moved to Wales she seemed to have found her ideal place, both spiritually and physically. Out in the countryside, at Little Wentwood Farm, she could ride her horse, feed her chickens and look after her sheep; she could sit and write in the little wooden house that her devoted husband of 39 years, Walt, had created for her, looking down the valley to Usk and the gleam of the sea beyond on a clear day, with the pond which he had also created just below her so that she could observe the newts, the frogs, the birds, the dragonflies – all the small creatures that recur in her poems. For Anne had an extraordinary eye for small things – the shape of a wing, the colour of an insect's back, the iridescence of a leaf. She watched, observed, took notes about the natural world around her, seeing when the swallows started to line up on the telegraph wires in readiness for their autumn migration, when the tadpoles started to fatten, looking for clues in the grass of the presence of living creatures, then turning her eyes upwards and watching the movement of the stars and planets from fields uncontaminated by the light pollution of a modern city . That meticulous, attentive observation is the thread that runs through all her poetry. In 'Magnolia' she writes:

> I have watched for weeks, just how dawn flings down a hint
> of shade from the top of the hill, a sway and flicker
> of distant pine, then foxglove, elder, blackthorn
> at a widening angle.

While in 'Yellow Meadow-Ants in Hallowed Ground' she introduces herself as an active agent in the insect world:

> I need to displace myself. I need to see,
> when the tip of my finger disturbs the alignment of dust
> over their open holes, how a human hand
> might seem (as to them) nothing more than the foot of a vole.

In a beautiful obituary for Anne, Meic Stephens quotes from an interview with her in which she said 'Poetry is my country'. But if poetry was her true country,

Wales came a close second, particularly the borderlands in which she had come to live. Anne and I first bonded through a shared sense of being border people, since neither of us could ever answer the elementary question 'Where are you from?' because to answer always required an explanation about our nomadism. In Wales, in the Welsh borders, she found a place and a people that she, as a bilingual, a woman born in Belgium, with an Irish passport and a mixed heritage could feel at home with. Earlier this year, when I was writing an Afterword for a forthcoming book on literature and religion, Anne corrected one of my sentences because I had referred to her as bilingual in English and French. No, she said, change that to French and then English, so as to convey the order of language acquisition that mattered so much to her.

Anne was, in many ways, not only my dear friend but my mentor. I would never have published any poetry had it not been for her encouragement and hard-hitting criticism. We spent hours and hours talking, we recommended books to one another, we sent one another drafts of our work. I have read hundreds of her poems in their early stages, and many years ago I translated parts of *Double Helix* into Italian. Translation is, of course, one of the most powerful ways of really getting to grips with another writer, because the translator has first of all to be a careful reader, before then endeavouring to recreate that writer's words anew. Anne and I liked the idea of Octavio Paz, that creating poetry and translating poetry are twin processes: in the first case, the poet sets down the signs in what he or she hopes will be an immutable form, while the task of the translator is to 'liberate' those signs and free them into another language.

Although Anne was not entirely sure about the 'immutable form', rather she believed that every version of a poem, even the final published one was simply one more draft. 'You can always go on tinkering' was how she put it. Through her, I started to think about the importance of drafts and the absurdity of the idea of a definitive reading, through her I discovered stylistics, through her I read R.S. Thomas and reread Henry Vaughan as a mature reader, not as a student, through her I read and met with a whole range of Welsh women poets, through her I discovered the beautiful work of Esther de Waal, another writer of the Borderlands, through her I learned to cope with loss by reading the Epic of Gilgamesh, which is the millennial poem about coming to terms with death. I cannot enumerate what I learned from Anne, and whenever I went to stay with her and Walt, she would have laid out another few books for me beside my bed that she thought might interest me. The last books included a couple of anthologies of Max Sebald's poetry and Mimi Khalvati's collection of translations of Fado poetry from the Portuguese.

Anne was that rare being, a creative artist with the eye of a scientist. She saw no gap between science and the arts, or between science and religion. Responding to the question of whether it is still possible to write a religious poem in the twenty-first century, she was, as ever, forthright in her views:

> I suppose I am suggesting that it must have been possible even in pre-history to experience sacred awe and to communicate it through actions, made objects, words-even before words came to be written. If a 'religious' poem is understood to be a poem which embodies or seeks after such experience, then it would surely be inaccurate to claim that, in any century whatever, a religious poem cannot be written-much less the twenty-first century, when the intricate wonders of the universe have come to be understood more deeply than ever before.

No opposition then, between religion and science, rather the belief that scientific discoveries enhance the sense of what she calls sacred awe. Science, like religion, for Anne were all about seeking to know the unknown, striving to overcome doubt. I was not at all surprised that she gradually moved into the Society of Friends, even as I moved back into the rituals of Roman Catholicism. Here too, our friendship moved us on parallel lines, so that we could talk about our spirituality and share our thoughts, while acknowledging differences.

Here on my desk, I have her final poems, carefully printed out as she always did (neither of us totally trusted computers to keep work safe), with her hand-written changes as she tinkered with what she had written. One is simply entitled 'What is it?' and the first line expands that question:

> What is it, when it starts- a poem?

For Anne, a poem was a process of discovery, a journey led by words into the unknown:

> words pull the mind after,
> gently, letting each phrase
> test, like a foot, the rope
>
> over an abyss, an abyss of silence,
> of missed awareness, of some
> as yet undiscovered thing.

Then when the words 'seem right', the fear of failure disappears, the rope sways:

'only the line in focus, the gulf below
a wonder that made this possible.

The idea of words bridging an abyss of silence is typical Cluysenaar. For her, poetry was as much part of everyday life as mucking out the hens and feeding the animals, but it was also always a mystical experience, since following words into the unknown led her to look more closely at the world around her, at her own past, at the prospect of death and at the Unknowable. Throughout her poetry there is a fascination with patterns, from the shape of a pot or a flower to the structure of DNA, from clouds and star formations to the wings of a butterfly or a beetle. There is also a fascination, which takes her again and again into the mystical, with what I can only term traces, from signs of man's existence back in unremembered time to the tracks in the soil overnight left by some small creature. That preoccupation with tracks and traces increased in her later poetry, though it was always there from the earliest collections. Latterly, her decision to write a sequence of diary poems led, in my personal view, to her finest poetry of all. The first volume of those diary poems, *Touching Distances* came out earlier this year. These are very personal poems, about her every day experiences – what she read, what she saw, a gift from a friends, the death of a friend, a childhood memory. For me, the most beautiful poem in that collection is the one from March 26, 2012, written just after her much loved cob, Pip, had fallen and broken his back. Anne knelt beside him for several hours waiting for the vet to come and put him down, and when she sent me this poem in draft form I wept. It is not remotely self-indulgent: she starts the poem with a concrete image, the moment when she saw the trace of her dead horse's hoof preserved in some dry soil. This 'dry clod', which recalls, probably unconsciously, the clay of Genesis, the 'precise cast of some step he took' takes her back to the dying horse, but then the word-journey that becomes the final verse moves on to something that now, in the aftermath of Anne's own death, I read with even deeper emotion:

> Just before he died, unable to lift
> even his head, he galloped in air–
> the eye I could see wide all at once,
> looking for the world, not finding it.

Here too, Anne writes about death as a seeking, involving a leap of the imagination. Pip gallops in air, even at the instant when he can no longer see the world he is still trying to look for. In her writing about death and the great question as to whether there is anything beyond death, Anne was deeply influenced by Henry Vaughan, whose poetry she edited in 2004. She was instrumental in creating the Vaughan Society, and in the work of Vaughan and his twin brother, Thomas, she found two seventeenth – century kindred spirits. In what is probably his best known poem of all, 'The World', Vaughan begins with an astonishing Image:

> I saw Eternity the other night
> Like a great *Ring* of pure and endless light,
> All calm, as it was bright,
> And round beneath it, Time in hours, days years
> driv'n by the spheres
> like a vast shadow move'd . . .

Eternity as great ring of endless light has echoes that are both religious and scientific. In his final verse, he writes how some who did weep and sing, and sing and weep 'soar'd up into the *Ring*'. When I think of Anne now, I like to think of her as one of those singers who soared up into the great Ring of Eternity, whose wide-open eyes can never be dazzled by the calm of that endless light.

CONTRIBUTORS TO THIS ISSUE

SAM ADAMS's publications include three books of poems and the novel Prichard's Nose (Y Lolfa, 2010). He edited Roland Mathias's Collected Poems and Collected Short Stories, and contributes a regular 'Letter from Wales' to the *Carcanet* magazine PN Review.

ALEX BARR's latest publication is *Take a Look at Me-e-e!* a book of stories for children (Pont Books 2014) based on 18 years living on a smallholding in West Wales. His most recent poetry collection is *Henry's Bridge* (Starborn 2006).

RICHARD BERENGARTEN's contributions to this issue belong to his latest book, *Notness* (Shearsman, 2015), a sequence of 100 sonnets. The title, an anagram of 'sonnets', could suggest that the 'core' of *isness* is *notness*, just as that of *notness* is *isness*: a never-ending dance.

PATRICK BOND lives in Lewes, Sussex. He is poet in residence on the Railway Land nature reserve. His inspiration is John Clare, poet of nature and of the open heart. Thomas Traherne, the *Gawain*-poet, Gerard Manley Hopkins and Geoffrey Hill are mainspring influences.

ALISON BRACKENBURY was born in 1953. Her latest collection is *Then* (Carcanet, 2013). Her ninth collection will be published by Carcanet in Spring 2016. New poems can be read at her website, www.alisonbrackenbury.co.uk.

ANNE CLUYSENAAR (1936-2014) published significant collections between 1982 and 2014, such as *Timeslips* (Carcanet, 1997), *Batu-Angas: Envisioning Nature with Alfred Russel Wallace* (Seren, 2008), *Water to Breathe* (Flarestack), *Migrations* (Cinnamon, 2011) and her most recent collection of diary poems, *Touching Distances* (Cinnamon, 2014). Anne helped to found the Vaughan Association and its journal, *Scintilla,* and was poetry editor for issues 1-15. She selected and introduced *Henry Vaughan Selected Poems* in the Golden Age of Spiritual Writing series, SPCK.

OLIVER COMINS lives and works in West London. Recent work has appeared in *Poetry Review, The North* and *The Rialto*. A short collection (*Yes to Everything*) won a Templar Portfolio Pamphlet Award in 2014 and will be published shortly.

KAY COTTON lives in rural Normandy where she is preparing her first full collection. Her poems have been published in Magazines and Anthologies including *Scintilla, The Rialto, Envoi,* 'The Book of Love and Loss', 'A Speaking Silence' and 'Her Wings of Glass'.

CLARE CROSSMAN lives outside Cambridge and has published in anthologies for Magdelene and Kettles Yard. *The Shape of Us* and *Vanishing Point* are from Shoestring Press. She is writing a monograph about artist Lorna Graves and a new collection.

MICHAEL CURTIS's Isle of Man collection, *Horizon*, was launched at the 2012 Manx Litfest and his twelfth poetry collection, *The Fire in Me Now*, was published by Cultured Llama in 2014. A pamphlet sequence, *Lullaby Days*, is due from Indigo Dreams this year.

CHRIS DODD has, for the last decade, lived in Trinidad, Canada and the USA. He now lives back in the UK. He is a poetry editor for the Canadian magazine *Freefall*. A pamphlet of his poems will be published this year in the UK by Smiths Knoll.

K. E. DUFFIN's poetry has appeared in *Agenda, Agni, The Cincinnati Review, Harvard Review, Ploughshares, Poetry, Poetry Salzburg Review, Prairie Schooner, The Sewanee Review, Shenandoah, The SHOp, Thrush, Verse*, and other journals. *King Vulture*, a book of poems, was published by the University of Arkansas Press.

RHIAN EDWARDS's first collection *Clueless Dogs* (Seren) won Wales Book of the Year 2013, the Roland Mathias Prize for Poetry 2013 and Wales Book of the Year People's Choice 2013. It was also shortlisted for the Forward Prize for Best First Collection 2012.

ROSE FLINT is a writer and artist. She has worked as a poet in healthcare for 20 years and taught Creative Writing for Therapeutic Purposes for Metanoia. A prize-winning poet, her fifth collection, *A Prism for the Sun* is forthcoming from Oversteps in 2015.

KATE FOLEY's most recent poetry publications are the collection *One Window North*, the long narrative poem *A Fox Assisted Cure* (from Shoestring Press, 2012) and the prizewinning title poem for *The Other Side of Sleep*, narrative poems from Arachne Press, 2014.

JOHN FREEMAN's taught for many years at Cardiff University. His most recent collection is *White Wings: New and Selected Prose Poems* (Contraband, 2014). Others include *A Suite for Summer* (Worple), and *The Light Is Of Love, I Think: New and Selected Poems* (Stride). www.johnfreemanpoetry.co.uk

PHILIP GROSS won the T.S.Eliot Prize 2009 and Wales Book of The Year 2010. A Fold In The River, a collaboration with artist Valerie Coffin Price, is due from Seren in March 2015, and a new collection, Love Songs of Carbon, from Bloodaxe in September.

DAVID HART, born in Aberystwyth, lives in Birmingham. He was previously a university chaplain, then arts administrator. His (Bardsey Island) *Crag Inspector* is available still from him (djhart11@mac.com), his *Library Inspector* is forthcoming from Nine Arches Press.

RICHARD HAWTREE is a medievalist living in Surrey currently writing a guide to the tenth-century *Exeter Book* manuscript. His poems have appeared in British and Irish literary magazines, most recently in *Weyfarers* and *The Penny Dreadful*.

JEREMY HOOKER is Emeritus Professor of English at the University of South Wales, and a Fellow of the Welsh Academy, and a Fellow of The Learned Society of Wales. His most recent book is *Openings: A European Journal* (Shearsman, 2014). His new collection of poems, *Scattered Light*, will be published by Enitharmon this year. He has published extensively on British and American poetry and the literature of place and Welsh writing in English, and his books include *Imagining Wales: A View of Modern Welsh Writing in English* (University of Wales Press, 2001).

W. D. JACKSON lives in Munich. His books of poetry, *Then and Now – Words in the Dark* and *From Now to Then* are published by Menard Press and *Boccaccio in Florence* by Shearsman. *A Giotto Triptych* and *Afterwords* appeared from Shoestring in 2014.

MAUREEN JIVANI has an MPhil from Glamorgan University. Mulfran Press published her pamphlet, *My Shinji Noon*. Her first full length collection *Insensible Heart* (Mulfran Press, 2009) was shortlisted for the London Fringe Festival Poetry Award 2010.

JOHN KILLICK is Poet Mentor for two projects at the Courtyard Centre for the Arts in Hereford. He recently edited the Selected Poems of Anna Adams for Shoestring Press. His latest book in the dementia field was 'Dementia Positive' for Luath Press in Edinburgh.

BRENDA LEALMAN is a prizewinner in the Bridport and Poetry Business Competitions. She has published in various journals including *Reactions, Scintilla, Studia Mystica* (USA). Her collections are *Nought at the Pole* (Flarestack, 1997), and *Time You Left* (Smith / Doorstop, 2000).

ANNA LEWIS's debut poetry collection, *Other Harbours*, was published in 2012 by Parthian. Recent poems have appeared in journals including *Agenda* and *The Lampeter Review*.

PATRICIA MCCARTHY is editor of *Agenda* poetry journal. Her work is published in many poetry journals in the UK, Ireland, the U.S. Two recent collections are *Rodin's Shadow* (2013) and *Horses between our Legs* (2014). She won the National Poetry Competition in 2013.

SEAN H. MCDOWELL is Director of the University Honors program at Seattle University and editor of the *John Donne Journal*. His poems have appeared most recently in *The Lyric*; *Clover, a literary rag*; *Vine Leaves Literary Journal*; and *The Best of Vine Leaves Literary Journal 2014*.

HELEN MOORE is an award-winning ecopoet. Her debut collection, *Hedge Fund, And Other Living Margins* (Shearsman Books, 2012) will be followed by *ECOZOA*, described by John Kinsella as "a milestone in the journey of ecopoetics", published by Permanent Publications (March 2015).

JONATHAN NAUMAN is Secretary of the Vaughan Association (USA). His note on "Henry Vaughan's *The Mount of Olives*, Henry Francis Lyte, and 'Abide With Me'" appeared recently in *Notes and Queries*, and his essay "Old Forest and Barrow Downs: A Natural Prelude to *The Lord of the Rings*" will be published this year in *Hither Shore*.

ROBERT NISBET was Associate Lecturer in Creative Writing at Trinity College, Carmarthen. His poems appear in magazines like *The Frogmore Papers*, *The Interpreter's House*, *Dream Catcher* and *The Journal*, and in his collection *Merlin's Lane* (Prolebooks, 2011).

CHRIS NORRIS teaches Philosophy at Cardiff University. He has written many academic books as well as a volume of poetry, *The Cardinal's Dog*, published by De La Salle University Press, 2013. A second collection, *The Winnowing Fan and Other Verse-Essays*, is forthcoming from Bloomsbury.

ALAN PAYNE was born in Trinidad and lives in Sheffield. His pamphlet *Exploring the Orinoco* was a winner in the 2009 – 10 Poetry Business Competition. He has had poems published in *Smiths Knoll*, *The North* and *Scintilla*, and in various anthologies.

CHRIS PREDDLE has retired from libraries to a green valley below the Pennines in West Yorkshire. His second collection is *Cattle Console Him* (Waywiser, 2010); his first was *Bonobos* (Biscuit, 2001). He is translating Sappho's poems and fragments.

NOAM REISNER is a senior lecturer in the department of English and American Studies at Tel Aviv University. He is author of *Milton and the Ineffable* (Oxford, 2009) and *John Milton's Paradise Lost: A Reading Guide* (Edinburgh, 2011) and has published on a wide range of topics in early modern literature, philosophy and theology. His interests include Marlowe, Shakespeare, Milton, Elizabethan and Jacobean drama, and the religious poetry and prose of the 16th and 17th centuries.

LESLEY SAUNDERS has published several books of poetry and works with visual artists, dancers and musicians. These poems pay tribute to her youngest grandson, conceived by *in vitro* fertilisation. Lesley is a visiting professor at the Institute of Education, London.

THOMAS R. SMITH lives in western Wisconsin and teaches in Minneapolis. His books of poems include *The Glory* published this year by Red Dragonfly Press. He has also edited *Airmail: The Letters of Robert Bly and Tomas Tranströmer*, published by Bloodaxe in the UK.

JOCK STEIN is a poet, piper and preacher from East Lothian. He brings experience of the Sheffield steel industry, people and places in East Africa, and the life of modern Scotland to his poetry, which has taken off since his 70th birthday.

EDWARD STOREY lives near Presteigne, Powys. He was one of the prize winners of the Cardiff International Poetry Competition 2014 and his tenth collection, 'Seeing the Light', will be published by Leverett Press later this year.

SEÁN STREET is Emeritus Professor at Bournemouth University. Of nine collections his latest is *Cello* (Rockingham Press). Prose includes *The Poetry of Radio* and *The Memory of Sound* (Routledge). He has also authored books on Gerard Manley Hopkins (Souvenir Press) and The Dymock Poets (Seren).

REGINA WALTON's poetry has appeared in *Poetry East* and other journals. She has essays in the forthcoming volumes *George Herbert, Beauty, and Truth: New Essays on Herbert's Christian Aesthetic* and *Preaching and the Theological Imagination*. An Episcopal priest, Regina serves a parish in Newton, Massachusetts.

PHILIP WEST is Fellow and Tutor in English at Somerville College, Oxford, and 'Times' Lecturer in the Faculty of English. He is the author of *Henry Vaughan's Silex Scintillans: Scripture Uses* (Oxford: Oxford University Press, 2001) as well as articles on early modern devotional poetry and religion. His current project is a critical edition of *The Poems of James Shirley* for OUP.

ROBERT WILCHER was Reader in Early Modern Studies in the English Department at the University of Birmingham and is now an honorary Fellow of the Shakespeare Institute in Stratford-upon-Avon. He has published *Andrew Marvell* (CUP, 1985), *The Writing of Royalism 1628-1660* (CUP, 2001), *The Discontented Cavalier: The Work of Sir John Suckling in its Social, Religious, Political, and Literary Contexts* (University of Delaware Press, 2007), and various essays and books on Shakespeare, Milton, Marvell, Vaughan, Quarles, *Eikon Basilike*, Beckett, and other modern playwrights. He is one of three editors of a new complete works of Henry Vaughan for Oxford University Press.

CHARLES WILKINSON's recent work has appeared in *Poetry Wales*, *Poetry Salzburg*, *Tears in the Fence* and *Envoi*. A pamphlet, *Ag & Au*, came out Flarestack Poets in 2013. He helps to run the Red Parrot poetry events in Presteigne, Powys.

DOIRAN WILLIAMS was born in North Wales of Welsh parents. After the army he joined the government legal service. On retirement he was ordained an Anglican priest and lives in Hereford diocese.

MARGARET WILMOT was born in California and has lived in Sussex since 1978, drawn by imaginative associations . . . memory, landscape, ideas, paintings, words – seeing where the pencil leads, exploring. A pamphlet has been published by Smiths Knoll entitled *Sweet Coffee*.

HOWARD WRIGHT lectures at the Belfast School of Art. His first collection, 'King of Country' was published by Blackstaff Press in 2010. Templar Press produced 'Blue Murder' in 2011. Recent poems have appeared in the Shop, Dark Horse and Stand.

THE ARTIST

EMIKO AIDA is a printmaker and painter living in London. She was born in Jindajii, Tokyo, a town with a Japanese temple dedicated to the Water God, several Buddhist temples and Christian Monasteries. She is a member of Royal Society of Painter-Printmakers. Her work is exhibited in over 10 galleries through out the U.K., the U.S.A. and Japan and in many private, public and corporate collections including the New York Public Library, USA and Guangdong Museum of Art, China. The prizes she has been awarded include: the 1982 and '83 Japan University of Print-making Purchase Prize, Tokyo, the 1989 L`Escargot Restaurant Award in Royal College of Art, London, the 1997 The Nordstern Award in Royal Academy of Arts, London, Purchase prize from the 16th SPACE International Print Biennial in Seoul, Korea, the 2014 Vivien Leigh Bequest Prize, Ashmolean Museum, Oxford, and Word Thomas Award, 2nd prize at the 2014 National Open Competition. She teaches Printmaking at The Hampstead School of Art. Her works are featured in a book, "Printmakers Today" published by Schiffer Publishing (USA). She can be reached at Studio 1, Unit 2&4, ACAVA, 11 Colville Road, London W3 8BL, or www.aidastudios.com.

The cover image is *Happy kitty.*

5269644R00112

Printed in Germany
by Amazon Distribution
GmbH, Leipzig